# RECIPES FOR TIRED TEACHERS

## Well-Seasoned Activities for the ESOL Classroom

Contributed by teachers associated with
Pilgrims Language Courses, Canterbury, England

Edited by Christopher Sion

ADDISON-WESLEY PUBLISHING COMPANY, INC.

## A Publication of the World Language Division

Christopher Sion has taught English to speakers of other languages in England, Spain, the Canary Islands, Austria, and Germany, and has contributed to journals, professional books, and dictionaries. He holds degrees from the University of Cape Town and the University of Keele and has also studied at the International Language Centre in London, the Goethe Institute in West Berlin, and Huddersfield Polytechnic.

Since 1979 Mr. Sion has also been active in the field of teacher training and has conducted programs and seminars in England, Germany, and Belgium.

Dedicated to all those language students
throughout the world who are just sitting
there in class . . .

Publisher's Staff

Editorial: Talbot F. Hamlin, Jacqueline Oakes

Production/Manufacturing: James W. Gibbons

Illustrations by Laura Maine and Beth Anderson

Cover and text design by Bonnie Chayes Yousefian

ISBN 0-201-06509-6

25 26 27 28 29 30 -CRS- 020100

# NTRODUCTION

*Recipes for Tired Teachers* is a collection of classroom tested teaching activities for students of English as a second or foreign language. Created by more than 40 teachers all over the world and tested and refined in their classrooms, the collection contains such exercises as role simulations, group dynamics activities, language games, creativity exercises; and ideas for business English, for collecting feedback, for imaginative conversation classes, and for listening, reading, and writing. Some activities will appeal especially to those interested in psychology, others to teachers who despair of teaching and reviewing vocabulary or breaking the ice with a new class. Some activities are centered on a linguistic function, such as interrupting, while others provide new, lively ways of dealing with a particular grammatical structure. All help develop speaking and listening skills. Recipes are provided for all learning levels. Most of them can be used with or adapted for any age group. The Table of Recipes on pages v-xii shows level, time required, language function(s), and other information about each recipe.

Because they are brief and self-contained, the recipes may be used in a variety of ways. They are especially helpful to the teacher whose class is "bogged down" and needs a change of pace or the teacher who must fill an empty half hour and rejects out of hand the kind of busy work too often used for this purpose. Creative teachers will find countless situations in which one or more of the recipes will enliven the class and stimulate and motivate the students.

The recipes are divided into eight units on the basis of their major emphasis. The division is not hard and fast. For example, although there is a unit called "Role Playing," not every recipe that uses role playing is placed there; some are in other units. Similarly, vocabulary is developed in many recipes in addition to those found in the unit called "Vocabulary." The final unit, "Fun and Games," includes activities that might easily have gone elsewhere, but are placed here because of their game structure.

Each recipe includes, at the top, the suggested time, the language function(s) developed, practiced, or reinforced, and the materials required. A section called "Before Class" describes preparations that must be made before the recipe is used. (This section is omitted if no specific preparation, other than familiarizing oneself with the recipe, is required.) The section called "In Class" presents, step by step, the procedure for using the recipe with the students.

All the recipes are designed for classroom use. It is assumed that the usual classroom fixtures will be available, including a chalkboard (referred to in the recipes as "the board") or its equivalent (flip chart, newsprint pad, overhead projector), and that students will have paper and pens or pencils. Accordingly, these are not included in the list of "Materials Needed" at the top of the recipe.

*Recipes for Tired Teachers* originated with activities suggested by teachers at the summer sessions of Pilgrims Language Courses held at the University of Kent in Canterbury, England. Because Pilgrims teachers come from all parts of the world, the recipes represent teaching experience gathered in many places—from Chile to China, from Korea to California, from Western Europe, the Middle East, Japan and Australia to Romania, Turkey, South Africa, and Brazil—the list goes on. The contributors' backgrounds, in addition to the fact that they all teach English to non-English-speaking persons, include modern languages, politics, philosophy, journalism, and industry. Their names appear at the end of the recipes they submitted.

The editor's task has been not only to select and classify the recipes, but also to establish a thread of cohesion in the style and format without losing the personal spark of each of the contributors. All the editor's changes have been made for one purpose only: to make the descriptions and instructions as clear as possible so that the ideas will be readily accessible to the select population of teachers whose rewarding job it is to help their students learn English.

The creative impulse of the teacher in bringing the activities to life is natural and should be encouraged. Just as a good cook does more than blindly follow a recipe, so a good teacher adds his or her own special flavoring to an activity. You should feel free to condense or expand, to adjust the language up or down, to change a pair activity to one for small groups, and so on. I sincerely hope that teachers who try these recipes will not simply rehash them, but will accept them as outlines and suggestions, to be modified and adapted to the needs and interests of their students, so that the process of teaching/learning truly becomes one of re-creation.

Sources for the activities have been cited wherever possible, although the problem of establishing originality persists. Responses from the contributors have been along such lines as "It grew out of a party game/workshop/article/misunderstanding, and as far as I know has not been developed in TEFL or TESL . . ." If a teacher modifies an article and demonstrates it in a seminar, where a colleague likes it, adapts it, and describes it to a student, who passes it on (including a few changes) to a friend, who in turn personalizes it and writes it up, who is to get the credit? As Gertrude Moscowitz observes in the Introduction to *Caring and Sharing in the Foreign Language Classroom* (Newbury House, 1978), "Tracking down . . . activities to their original source can be as difficult as determining the creators of folklore or legends. The origin of some exercises is not traceable; they just seem to be handed down." Any lack of proper acknowledgment in this book is unintentional.

I should like to thank Mario Rinvolucri and James Dixey of Pilgrims Language Courses in Canterbury and Mike Lavery and Martin Worth of the 3M Company in Neuss, West Germany, for help and encouragement; and, of course, the contributors for their contributions. A special word of thanks should also go to my London agent, Mr. A.R. Evans, for all his advice and assistance, and to Talbot F. Hamlin of Addison-Wesley for editorial suggestions and for guidance in the ways of American spelling and usage. A further acknowledgment goes to Saxon Menné for suggesting the title.

The final credit must go to my wife Kathleen for telling me to "get on with it" on those days when I came close to waiting yet another week (or two). Without her gentle pushing, the manuscript would almost certainly still be lying in the drawer.

*Christopher Sion*

# TABLE OF RECIPES

Including title, author, suggested level, approximate time, and materials needed. Language functions are in *italics*. General comments are in parentheses.

Language functions are in *italics*; general comments are in parentheses.    **v**

## Unit II—CREATIVE WRITING AND THINKING

## Unit III—READING AND WRITING

     Language functions are in *italics*; general comments are in parentheses.

## Unit IV—LISTENING

Language functions are in *italics*; general comments are in parentheses.

## Unit V—ROLE PLAYING

Language functions are in *italics*; general comments are in parentheses.

## Unit VI—STRUCTURES AND FUNCTIONS

Language functions are in *italics*; general comments are in parentheses.

# Unit VII—VOCABULARY (LEXIS)

## Unit VIII—FUN AND GAMES

Language functions are in *italics*; general comments are in parentheses.

Language functions are in *italics;* general comments are in parentheses.

# UNIT 1

GROUP DYNAMICS

# YOU ARE WHAT YOU WILL

## Unit I / GROUP DYNAMICS / Level: Intermediate and above / Time: 30—60 minutes

**Language Function(s):** Imagining; asking and answering questions

**Materials:** None

### In Class

1. Tell the class that they are to imagine another life. In this new life they can take the form of an animal, a plant, or an object. The one form they cannot take is that of a human being. Give them a few minutes to think about what they would like to be.

2. Then ask the students, one at a time, to tell what they are and to describe themselves. Encourage the other students to ask anything they like about the new personality, its function, background, feelings, and so on.

3. After the students have revealed and described their new identities, conduct a general feedback discussion. Help the students to analyze what they have learned about themselves and one another and about human aspirations in general. You may also want to elicit discussion of possible contrasts between the students' "new life" and "real life" identities in terms of such criteria as age, sex, nationality, or any others that may show up in the course of the lesson.

### Author's Note

Because it is impossible to tell in advance how long a given student may take, it is a good idea to have the students draw lots to determine the order in which they will give their descriptions. That way, no one will feel deliberately excluded if there is not time for all to present. In such a case, however, each student should be given the opportunity to name the object he or she has chosen and to say a couple of sentences about himself or herself.

*Sonia Taylor*

# NEIGHBORS

## Unit I / GROUP DYNAMICS / Level: Intermediate and above / Time: 50 minutes

**Language Function(s):** Describing, imagining

**Materials:** None

### In Class

1. Give each student a piece of paper. Tell the students that each one is to draw a house on his or her paper. They are to work alone. When the houses are drawn, they are to fold the papers in two so that the houses cannot be seen. The papers are collected, placed in the center of the table, and shuffled. Each student then picks one and unfolds it.

2. Now ask the students, one at a time, to describe in detail the house on the paper each has chosen. Ask them to describe the occupants of the house, the furniture in the house, the colors used in the different rooms, the location of the house, and any other details they can think of.

3. Next, arrange all the drawings face up on the table. Ask each student to choose one that he or she likes and write his or her name on the back of it. There should be only one name on each drawing.

4. Then have the class, working together, arrange the houses in groups of three. (If the number of drawings is not divisible by three, one or two groups may have four houses.) Let the students develop their own criteria for grouping the houses. Provide no more guidance than "houses that you think go together well."

5. When the sets of houses are formed, ask those whose names appear on the drawings to sit together and create a three-minute skit that illustrates or depicts the relationships among the "neighbors" who live in the three (or four) houses.

6. Have each group present its skit to the group.

*John Morgan*

# I-3 LYING: An Icebreaker

Unit I / GROUP DYNAMICS / Level: Low intermediate and above / Time: 30–40 minutes

**Language Function(s):** Disguising the truth; exchanging and comparing personal information

**Materials:** None

## In Class

1. Have the students form pairs. (If this activity is done at the beginning of the course as suggested, you may wish to assign the pairs yourself, since the students may not know one another and may feel bashful about pairing off.)

2. Tell the students they are to talk to their partners about themselves. One partner will talk while the other takes notes. Then they reverse roles. Tell them that they can reveal as much or as little about themselves as they like, but that *about three-quarters of what they say should be lies.*

3. Have the students repeat this process two or three times with different partners. Each time they meet a new partner, they give different information. However, the information should be about the same areas. In other words, they talk about the *same subjects* with each partner but tell *different lies* about these subjects to each partner.

4. Now have the students report back to the whole group about what they heard from each of their partners, using the notes they took in each interview as a guide. As each student reports, all those who met the same person listen carefully and then point out the discrepancies between the stories that person told. The fun comes in trying to decide what the truth really is, with everyone speculating about everyone else.

5. Each person finally tells the truth, leaving everybody knowing something about him or her.

## Author's Note

This exercise is intended as an icebreaker at the beginning of a new course, but could be used later in the course as well.

*Malachy Mulholland*

**Unit I / GROUP DYNAMICS / Level: Low intermediate and above / Time: 20–30 minutes**

**Language Function(s):** Asking questions; evaluating content; telling or disguising the truth

**Materials:** Pictures (see Method Two below)

## In Class

1. *Method One.* Tell a short anecdote which may either be true or be a complete fabrication. Have the group ask you questions about it. Give additional information as necessary to generate more questions. Then ask the students to decide whether you were telling the truth or making the whole thing up—lying, that is. Put it to a vote.

   *Method Two.* A variation is to bring in a picture (which the students cannot see) and describe it to the class. Again, the description may be true or it may be completely false. Let the group quiz you about the details. As with Method One, the students must decide whether you are telling the truth or lying.

2. To follow up, ask a student to tell a story or describe a picture in the same way. Again, the remainder of the class must decide whether the student is telling the truth or lying.

3. As an optional extra with either method, you may wish to ask students to explain why they voted as they did. This can be done individually, student by student, or by a panel of three or four students. Encourage the students to give contextual reasons for their verdicts rather than make comments such as ''(S)he always lies / exaggerates.''

## Authors' Note

For Method Two, it is a good idea to use an ''unlikely'' picture—perhaps even an abstract or surrealistic one—the first time you do this exercise. This will create an atmosphere in which the improbable is on a par with one's more ''normal'' expectations.

*Joan Hewitt*
*Christopher Sion*

# I-5 INFORMATION EXTRACTION

**Language Function(s):** Asking questions

**Materials:** None

## In Class

1. Divide the class into groups of three. One of the persons in each group is the questioner, another is the answerer, and the third is the umpire or referee.

2. Tell the questioner to write on a slip of paper something he or she wants to know about the answerer, and to give the slip to the umpire.

3. Now tell the questioner that his or her job is to extract the information on the slip from the answerer *without directly asking the question he or she has written down*. The umpire's job is to make sure that the questioner follows this rule and does not ask the question directly or change a question in midstream. To do this, the umpire can stop the questioner at any time. You may wish to give each questioner a time limit to expedite the exercise, or you may leave it to the group to impose, or not impose, a time limit.

4. When the questioner has extracted the information, or the time limit has been passed, the members swap roles or start again.

*William Atkinson*

**Language Function(s):** Interpreting visual stimuli; discussing personal perception

**Materials:**     Grid with drawings

## Before Class

Duplicate copies of the grid (see page 8). You may also want to copy figure 1 on the board or a piece of newsprint, but keep it covered until you are ready to use it (see Step 2).

## In Class

1. Distribute copies of the grid. Tell the students that they are to make a drawing in each of the twelve rectangles. Eleven of the rectangles have small figures in them. These figures are to be part of the drawings in those rectangles. Each drawing must be separate from the others: students may *not* combine two or more drawings to make one large drawing.

2. Once the drawings are complete, have the students write the following words on them in the corresponding squares (figure 1). If you have made a large copy of figure 1 as described (see *Before Class*), it can be uncovered at this time and students may copy the words from it.

Figure 1

| You | Others | God |
|---|---|---|
| Death | Gift to Yourself | Love |
| Security | You and Your Surroundings | Your Surroundings |
| Aspirations | Balance | Spirit |

3. Then give the class the following definitions or explanations of the words they have written on their drawings:

YOU—How you view yourself.

OTHERS—How you view other people.

GOD—Your view of religion.

DEATH—The way you regard death.

GIFT TO YOURSELF—Something you would like to give yourself.

LOVE—Your idea of love.

SECURITY—Your idea of security.

YOU AND YOUR SURROUNDINGS—How you see yourself in relation to your surroundings.

YOUR SURROUNDINGS—How you regard your surroundings.

ASPIRATIONS—The way you see your aspirations, aims, goals.

BALANCE—How you balance the forces in your life; your sense of (spiritual) balance.

SPIRIT—Your sense of spirit, energy, enthusiasm, liveliness.

4. Finally, divide the students into pairs to discuss their interpretations of their drawings and the ways in which these drawings could represent or correspond to the labels they wrote on them in Step 2.

## Author's Note

This exercise is an adaptation of part of the Wartegg Drawing Test.

*Carlos Maeztu*

# THE LAST TIME: An Encounter

## Unit I / GROUP DYNAMICS / Level: Intermediate / Time: 45 minutes

**Language Function(s):** Exchanging and comparing personal information

**Materials:** None

### In Class

1. Ask the students, one by one, to talk about some simple recent incident, such as the last time they paid a bill. Use questions such as: Where were they? How much was the bill? What was it for? Do they prefer cash or checks? Or ask about the last time they used the telephone. Did they make the call or receive it? Was it a business call or a private one? What was it about? Do they like using the phone? In which room is their phone at home? Which member of the family uses it most? Other similar incidents and questions can be used. Give enough time for the answerer to remember, but keep the pace brisk. Prompt with your own examples when necessary. Make it very clear that the "last time" element is just a lever to provoke discussion. If a student says he or she can't remember the last bill payment or phone call, or that it concerned something personal, ask him or her to talk about any recent example, or switch to another subject.

2. Collect a set of about 25 "last time" examples and write them on the chalkboard or a newsprint pad. Elicit as many as you can from the group, but be sure there is a good mix of everyday and personal items. A typical list might include:

   The last thing you bought
   The last joke you heard
   The last letter you wrote
   The last word you looked up
   The last class you attended
   The last present you gave

The last time you:
   shook hands
   entertained
   were surprised
   played a game
   ate out
   ate alone
   kissed someone
   felt depressed
   gave money to charity
   were angry
   made someone angry
   made a mistake
   had a practical joke played on you
The last time you:
   overslept
   went to church
   went to a film, a concert
   went to the theater, the zoo
   stayed in a hotel
   really laughed
   made (or broke) a promise
   told a lie
   were lied to
   fell (or didn't fall) into temptation
   played a practical joke

3. Divide the class into pairs and have each pair choose about 12 of the situations on the board to talk about. (If they wish, they may choose more and go into less detail on them, or fewer and spend more time on each; the decision is theirs.)

4. Let the pairs discuss the points they have chosen.

### Author's Note

By making their own choices from the list, the members of each pair can decide what they want to focus on and how personal or distanced they want to be. Thus the exercise finds its own "level of openness" for each pair.

*Christopher Sion*

# WE'LL ANSWER FOR YOU

**Unit I / GROUP DYNAMICS / Level: Intermediate / Time: 20–40 minutes**

**Language Function(s):** Asking and answering personal questions

**Materials:** None

## In Class

1. Tell the group that you are ready to answer questions about yourself. Tell them they may ask fairly deep questions: they do not need to confine themselves to superficial questions such as "What are your hobbies?" Suggest that each student write ten questions he or she would like to ask.

2. As the students write their questions, circulate around the room, supplying words they are short of and helping with the formulation of questions as necessary. (Help students only with the most recent sentences they have written; if a student is composing question 7, a mistake in question 1 may be several light years behind him or her in emotional time.)

3. When everyone has written eight to ten questions, pick out those students with whom you feel the greatest empathy, those you believe will best be able to read and interpret you. Ask these students to sit in a crescent behind you, facing the rest of the group. Collect the questions from the group in the crescent and give them to the remainder of the class.

4. Now sit down facing the people with the questions and invite them to fire both their own questions and those of the people in the crescent at you. Tell them that the people in the crescent *are going to answer for you* and that you will remain silent.

   Deny the questioners eye contact, but silently react to the answers given by your "doubles" or "alter egos" behind you. It is important that the doubles should be able to "read your back"—to understand from subtle body-language cues how you react to the answers they give.

   The degree to which you concentrate on what is happening will strongly influence the power of the exercise.

5. Have a "debriefing" discussion with the group. How confident did the "doubles" feel in the answers they gave for you? Did their confidence increase or decrease as the questioning continued? How did the remainder of the group feel about the accuracy of the doubles' answers?

6. If there is time, and students are interested, you may want to repeat the exercise with another participant in the "hot seat."

## Author's Note

This exercise is best used early in a course, before students have very much factual knowledge about one another. But the mood of the group must be right for it: do not use the exercise with a group that is not ready for it.

The exercise is a variation of one proposed by John Morgan, in which members of a group ask a picture questions, while others in the group double for the picture. We learned the concept of "doubling" from Moreno's work in psychodrama. For my introduction to the application of psychodrama to language teaching, I have to thank Bernard Dufeu of Mainz University.

*Mario Rinvolucri*

**Unit I / GROUP DYNAMICS / Level: Intermediate and above / Time: 45 minutes**

**Language Function(s):** Discussing; justifying; expressing opinions and feelings

**Materials:**     Copies of cartoon figures (page 12)

## Before Class

Duplicate copies of the cartoon figures. You will need one copy for each class member plus at least one extra copy. Cut the extra copy into pieces so that there will be one character for each student except for one or two. For these students, prepare blank slips of the same size with the instructions, ''Say what you really think.''

## In Class

1. Distribute the cut-out slips to the students. Either give a deliberately selected apposite (or inapposite) cartoon to each student, or put all the slips into a hat or bag and let each student take one. (This random assignment of characters to students can relax some of the tensions the group may feel about expressing negative feelings.)

2. Tell the class that they have 10–15 minutes for a discussion, to be chaired by one of them. The dis-

cussion should concern the material they have been given, but no one should directly reveal the content of his or her piece of paper. Instead, students are to respond *in character*, but without actually quoting the words on their paper. During the discussion, circulate among the students, correcting and helping with vocabulary as necessary.

3. Stop the discussion after about fifteen minutes and pass out copies of the entire page of cartoon figures. Ask the class to identify which students were taking the parts of which cartoon characters and who was telling the truth—saying what he or she really thought. Ask students to justify their answers.

4. At this point, students frequently begin to clarify their attitudes. Select as a new chairperson one of the students who had drawn a slip marked ''Say what you really think'' and begin a fresh discussion in which people express their real feelings.

## Author's Note

Students will participate more honestly and vigorously in the genuine discussion (step 4) than they would without the use of steps 1, 2 and 3. *Discussion Tactic* is a good exercise to get a new or inhibited group to open up or to broach a ''danger topic'' such as how students really feel about the course. The cartoon characters and the sentences attributed to them can be adapted to elicit opinions on other sensitive topics.

*Joan Hewitt*

*Mr. A:* Why should I have to listen to other foreign students' mistakes? The teacher should talk most of the time.

*Miss B:* I just want to enjoy myself—fun and games for everyone!

*Miss C:* I hate serious discussions—politics for example. When people disagree there is a very unpleasant atmosphere in the class. Learning should be fun.

*Mr. D:* I like people—knowing another language means I can meet *more* people. Making mistakes isn't really important if I can communicate.

*Mr. E:* Most teachers talk too much and dominate the lesson.

*Mrs. F:* Actually I can learn more from a good textbook than from discussion groups and oral practice.

*Mr. G:* As an intellectual, I find language useful only to be polite or make social conversation in English.

*Miss H:* Don't ask me—the teacher knows best.

*Mr. I:* Grammar is necessary before everything else. Once you know it, *then* you can begin speaking.

# IS IT
# REALLY IMPORTANT?

**Unit I / GROUP DYNAMICS / Level: Lower intermediate and above / Time: 30–40 minutes**

**Language Function(s):** Comparing ideas; justifying decisions

**Materials:** None

## In Class

1. Divide the class into groups of about four to six students.

2. Ask the students, working as individuals, to write down five words that they associate with their group. These should be words that might have relevance for any of the group's members.

3. Have each group produce a combined list of all the words chosen by the group's members. Then ask them to cull the list by crossing out or discarding 20% of the words. Each group member should then make a personal copy of the culled list for use in step 4.

4. Working again as individuals, each student draws two columns next to the list of words. In the first column, next to each word, the student writes a number expressing the significance of the word to himself or herself. Numbers run from 0 to 10, with 0 indicating no importance and 10 indicating great importance. In the second column, the student rates each word for someone else in the group, using the same numbering system. For example, if "television" were the word, a student might rate it as 3 for him or herself, since he or she prefers reading, but might rate it as 8 for a group member he or she knew to be saving up for a new TV.

5. Compare and discuss the results. Were there words that were consistently chosen by all groups? Were there wide variations in the ratings? Can students explain why they rated some words high and others low? Can they justify their ratings of the supposed preferences of others?

## Author's Note

This exercise is intended for use with classes that have worked together long enough so that the students know a good deal about one another.

*John Morgan*

# I-11 FEELINGS AND PICTURES

**Language Function(s):** Expressing, describing, and discussing feelings

**Materials:** Reproductions of famous paintings in the form of slides (if possible), prints, or postcards; slide projector and screen (if slides are used)

## In Class

1. Discuss with the class how words can express or describe emotions. Brainstorm vocabulary of emotions and feelings, and ask each student to write down words or expressions that he or she feels confident to use or would like to experiment in using. Tell the class that you are going to give them the opportunity to use some of these words.

2. Display reproductions of several paintings. Use color slides if possible; otherwise use prints or, as a last resort, postcards. The paintings should preferably be lesser known works and/or works with ambiguous subject matter. Ask the students to write down their *feelings or impressions* as they see each painting. Be sure to allow adequate time for each picture.

3. Divide the class into small groups, and ask them to discuss their impressions and the vocabulary they have used to describe their feelings. Then ask each group to choose a picture and make up a title that sums up the group's feelings about it.

4. As a variation, you may wish to ask students to mime the feelings they had collectively for a picture. Each group is to guess, from the mimes, the identity of the other groups' pictures.

*Marjorie Baudains*

# INTUITING A PICTURE

**Unit I / GROUP DYNAMICS / Level: Advanced / Time: 30 minutes**

**Language Function(s):** Expressing feelings; describing

**Materials:** Original or reproduction of an emotive painting or photograph

## Before Class

Select an emotive picture; a copy of a painting or an artistic photograph usually works well. Consider the kinds of feelings the picture arouses in you and the attitude to reality it conveys. Bring the picture to class.

## In Class

1. Brainstorm vocabulary with the class. Guide the brainstorming into the general area of your feelings about the painting, but avoid actually using words that express your feelings so as not to direct students' own responses when they later see the picture.

2. Give the picture to one student without letting the others see it. Tell the student to describe the picture to the class, but to do so without mentioning anything in it. He or she must describe it purely in terms of the emotions it provokes. As the student describes the picture, have the rest of the class close their eyes and imagine a picture that fits the language they hear.

3. Then ask the students to discuss in pairs the kinds of pictures they imagined and make comparisons between them. Ask some of the students to describe their imagined pictures to the whole class.

4. Now show everyone the picture and ask for comments on it. Is it as they imagined it? Do they accept and agree with the first account of it in terms of feelings? Why or why not?

5. Finally, if the picture makes a specific point, it may be possible to start a discussion about that point.

*Randal Holme*

# I-13 PICKING A PICTURE

**Language Function(s):** Expressing feelings; explaining; justifying

**Materials:**    Reproductions of 20—30 paintings, all periods and styles

## Before Class

Secure 20—30 reproductions of paintings of all periods and styles and number each one.

## In Class

1. Lay the numbered pictures on the table, face up, and ask the students to each choose one they would like to talk about. Tell them they are not to reveal to you or to other students which picture they have chosen and they are not to remove it from the table.

2. Ask each student to write the names of the other students in the class, and next to each name write the number of the picture they believe that student will have chosen.

3. Now ask the students to come up one at a time and take the picture they chose. They should tell the class about their feelings toward it and explain why they selected it. If more than one student has cho-sen the same picture, each may retrieve it from the one before and hold it up while explaining his or her choice.

4. After a particular student has explained his or her choice, the rest of the class should:

   a. say which picture they thought the student would choose, and why;
   b. give their own feelings about the picture that was chosen.

   You may want to make a chart on the board for Step 4a.

5. Conduct a "debriefing" session in which you elicit discussion of the reasons for differences in taste and the connections between the way people speak and behave and the kinds of art they select. Take care to see that this discussion is free of personal in-nuendo.

## Author's Note

This idea developed from seeing a demonstration of Randal Holme's *Intuiting a Picture* (recipe I-12).

*David Hill*

# UNIT 2

# CREATIVE WRITING AND THINKING

# IDENTIFICATION PARADE

II-1

**Language Function(s):** Describing and identifying

**Materials:**     Portraits from magazines; drawing paper

## Before Class

Cut out interesting portraits (photographs of ordinary people) from magazines, as many as there are members of the class plus at least seven additional portraits. If possible, some of them, although of different people, should be similar in detail. Mount two of the portraits on large sheets of drawing paper so that vocabulary can be written around them. These two portraits should be full-page size if possible, so that they can be seen by the whole class. Attach one of the mounted portraits to the wall or so that it is clearly visible to all the students.

## In Class

## Method One (with written responses)

1. Call attention to the mounted portrait, and start a discussion about it. Allow the students to supply as much vocabulary descriptive of the portrait as they can without your help. As each term is introduced, write it, or have the person who introduced it write it on the paper surrounding the portrait. Help with any new words students are struggling to put across. Depending on the level, you may wish to introduce new ways of talking about such items as age, hair color, complexion, and so on. Add these to the words surrounding the portrait, but avoid turning the exercise into a glossary of new lexical terms. Include only words that you believe will be reused.

2. Now put up the second mounted portrait and repeat the process with it.

3. Explain to the students that they are each going to receive a portrait of a person who is suspected of a petty crime such as shoplifting. The students are witnesses to the crime and must give an accurate description in writing of the person they saw commit it—that is, the person whose portrait they have. Then hand out the portraits, telling the students not to show their portrait to anyone else in the class. Give them time to write their descriptions. The descriptions should be on separate paper, *not* on the portraits.

4. When the students have finished writing their descriptions, collect the pictures. Ask the students to exchange descriptions so that each has the description written by another. Tell them to read their new descriptions and think about the person described.

5. While the students are reading the new descriptions, shuffle the portraits and add the remaining five. Lay the shuffled portraits on the table face up, or put them up on the wall or chalkboard. Then ask the students to come up and identify the suspects, based on the descriptions they have read. When they believe they have spotted the "right person," they should check with the writer of the description to make sure they are correct.

6. You may wish to take the activity one step further and ask students why they were so sure that the picture they chose was correct.

## Method Two (no written responses)

1. and 2. These are the same as with Method One.

3. Give portraits to half of the students. These will be the witnesses. The other students will be detectives. Each witness will have a detective partner to whom he or she must give an oral description of the picture. (Obviously, the detective must not be able to see the picture.) The detectives may take notes of the witnesses' descriptions and then, after the portraits have been collected, shuffled, and laid on the table or put up on the wall (as in Step 5 of Method One), they must identify the suspects from the witnesses' descriptions.

## Author's Notes

Mary Gabriel has suggested the following variation to this activity: Each student writes a description of another member of the class. The descriptions, with no identification, are put up on the wall and the students then come up and read them. After reading a description, each student writes under it the name of the person he or she believes is described. When all the guesses have been made and explained the authors reveal the identities of the persons. It is safest to restrict the descriptions to physical characteristics and to *use the exercise with caution* and only with very well knit groups.

I should like to acknowledge the influence of Maley and Duff's *Drama Techniques in Language Learning* and Johnson and Morrow's *Approaches*, both published by Cambridge University Press.

*Sandra Moulding*

**Unit II / CREATIVE WRITING AND THINKING / Level: Low intermediate and above / Time: 40 minutes**

**Language Function(s):** Imagining and narrating

**Materials:** Small pictures of people, each mounted on blank writing paper, one for each student

## In Class

1. Divide the class into groups of five to ten students and ask each group to form a circle. Distribute a picture to each student.

2. Now ask each student to give his or her picture a name, and write it on the paper under the picture. The student then passes the picture to the person on his or her right who adds the age and occupation, and again passes it to the student at the right. The following details are completed the same way, one being added by each student who then passes it to the next student:

   —marital status and size of family

   —address

   —hobbies and interests (one or two of each)

   —one thing the person loves

   —one thing the person hates

   Keep the pace brisk and ask students to keep each contribution to one sentence. Give the class a few minutes to look at the completed sheets.

3. Now that the basic facts have been given (imagined) about the people in the pictures, suggest that the class might try imagining following them around on a typical day in their lives. What did they do yesterday? Tell the class to write a narrative account in the simple past, beginning their first sentence with

"Yesterday," and passing the pictures, this time to the left, after each student's contribution has been made. For this narrative, contributions should be limited to two sentences. The story for each character ends when the paper returns to the student who made the first contribution. (With very small groups and/or very eager students, you may wish to let the story make a second round.)

4. Let the students share the various accounts during the remainder of the class. At the end of class, collect the pictures and accounts; they can serve as the source of a list of common errors to be worked on the following day.

5. A possible follow-up is to continue using the characters, building more and more information into their stories, perhaps even to the point of making them alter egos for the students.

6. An alternate to Steps 3—5 is to have each student choose one of the characters built up in Step 2 and role play that character extemporaneously in one or more given situations. Some situations that might be used are: all the characters meet in an airport lounge or at a concert, all are arrested and placed in the same cell, all stand in line at a supermarket checkout. The students may think of others.

*Lou Spaventa*

# IMPRESSIONISTIC WRITING FROM PICTURES II-3

**Unit II / CREATIVE WRITING AND THINKING / Level: Low intermediate and above / Time: 45 minutes**

**Language Function(s):** Expressing feelings; writing poetry

**Materials:** An emotion-packed picture

## Before Class

Obtain an emotionally compelling picture, one that you believe will stir the emotions of the class. It may be strong and immediate or mysterious and elusive. It may be a reproduction of a painting or it may be a photograph. It should be large enough so that the whole class can see it when it is put up on the wall or board. Bring it to class but do not show it until Step 5.

## In Class

1. Introduce to the class the idea of free writing—writing without thinking about the mechanics, such as punctuation and syntax. You might compare it to "free form" in abstract painting or perhaps to the "automatic writing" of a psychic.

2. Then write on the board the names of two or three emotions, such as anger, joy, hate, loneliness, love, jealousy. Be sure that your list includes some of the "negative" emotions: these often produce a more immediate response than the more positive ones. Tell the students they are going to free-write about emotions. They may choose those they wish to write about: ask them if there are others that should be added to the list on the board, and accept their suggestions.

3. Now write an impressionistic "poem" on the board, associating whatever words and phrases come into your head in connection with one or more of the emotions whose names you have listed. The train of association will produce words and images that are disconnected; these should be laid out on the board in lines as in a free verse poem.

4. Now ask the students to write a "poem" of their own as you have done. (It does not matter if your poem influences those of the students. It is essential that you write one first to give the class confidence and to show them the kind of thing they are to do; it also forms a relationship between you and the class in doing the task. Nor does the teacher's poem inhibit the class at all.) After a minute or two, erase your poem while the students continue to write their own.

5. Now introduce the class to the picture you have brought. Ask them to write about it in just the same way they have written about the emotion words. Encourage the students, but do not pressure them. Tell them that it does not matter how they begin, and that once the first few words are on paper, things usually seem to flow. Urge them to use words that tell what the picture means to them. Tell them you are going to be writing your own poem while they are writing theirs.

6. Write your own poem, either on paper or on the board. If you write on the board, wait until they are well into their own work first.

7. Have students read their poems, and discuss them, comparing the different meanings they found in the picture. Finally, collect the poems into an anthology and duplicate it for the students. Keep a copy of the anthology to show to people who tell you it can't be done!

## Author's Note

Having the teacher write with the students is one of the best ways of encouraging reluctant students to write; it should be used when possible in any writing lesson.

*Don Salter*

# II-4 DVERTISEMENTS

**Language Function(s):** Persuading

**Materials:**     Advertisements cut from magazines; advertisement headlines cut from magazine ads; pictures of various kinds cut from magazines or newspapers; tape or cassette recorder

## In Class

1. Give each student a copy of a magazine advertisement. Ask the students to comment on what is being sold and on how the advertisement tries to catch the reader's eye and persuade him or her to buy.

2. Then give each student a headline from another advertisement. Avoid duplication: each student should have a separate headline to work with, different from those of the other students.

3. Put the pictures face up on the table and let each student choose one that he or she can relate to the headline, thus creating an advertisement.

4. Give the students about ten minutes to complete their ads, writing further copy as needed, and practicing reading their ads orally for a presentation. (Lower levels may need a little longer.) As they work, circulate around the room acting as language consultant but not as idea person. A thesaurus and a few dictionaries strategically placed will help deflect many of the vocabulary questions.

5. When the students have finished, ask them one at a time to read their advertisements in an expressive, persuasive, and entertaining manner, trying to attract and interest the listeners. If possible, tape the students as they make their presentations. The recording can then be played back, first straight through and then with pauses to give the group an opportunity to comment on what they hear.

6. As a variation, students may hide their pictures until they have completed their presentations. The surprise value of the pictures when shown after the presentation keeps interest high and provokes laughter and comment.

*Lou Spaventa*

# IMAGING

**Unit II / CREATIVE WRITING AND THINKING / Level: Intermediate and above / Time: 30 minutes**

**Language Function(s):** Making suggestions and associations

**Materials:** Small object(s) for which uses are to be imagined

## In Class

1. Bring in a simple, everyday object such as a cake tin, a large envelope, or a paper clip. Tell the class that they are to think of as many uses as possible for the object. A rectangular cake or bread tin, for example, could be used for storing pencils or other small objects, but you could also put wheels on it and use it for a skateboard (as suggested by one student for a metal candy box). The more imaginative the responses the better. It is important not to reject any: to do so could block other suggestions that students might have.

2. The students can work individually, in pairs, or in small groups. Give them a few minutes to think and discuss, and then go around the class, collecting their contributions. Ask students to explain their uses if necessary, but try not to interrupt the rhythm. Encourage them to use structures like "It could (might) be used as a . . ." but do not interrupt if students' imaginations are working productively.

3. Next have the class do a word association, either with the name of the original object or with one of the words that has come up frequently in the discussion of uses. Ask students to give as many associations as they can with the key word. Accept all associations even if they seem remote: the purpose is to generate imaginative associations.

4. Now select a word that has come up in Step 2. It should be something concrete and easy to visualize: for example, if the original object was an envelope,

an appropriate word might be "stamp" (if envelopes had been suggested for keeping stamps in). Tell the students to close their eyes and form a picture in their minds of the word you have chosen. Tell them to picture it within a frame or on a screen but to imagine that it is moving within that area.

5. Ask a member of the class to describe what he or she is visualizing. Then move to another student, asking him or her to continue, then another student, and so on, to build up a group fantasy. Prompt as necessary with questions such as, "What color is it?", "What's happening?", "What does it look like now?", "Has it changed?", or "What is it doing now?" Emphasize the visual aspect in your questions: you want the student to tell you what he or she is "seeing."

6. A useful variation for Steps 1 and 2 is to hold an initial group session with the entire class and then divide the group into pairs. Let them continue suggesting uses to each other, taking turns as in a game, with the rule that each one can stop the other by simply saying "Stop!" and then make his or her own contribution(s).

7. Finally, return to the original object you brought in and rethink possible uses of it.

8. For more advanced classes, an interesting follow-up is to investigate the whole issue of convergent and divergent thinking. A reference librarian can direct

you to sources; one such is *Contrary Imaginations* by Liam Hudson (Pelican). Another is *The Nature of Human Intelligence* by J.P. Guilford (McGraw-Hill). Students might be interested in investigating such questions as how convergent and divergent thinking vary with persons of different ages, sexes, and occupations, divergent thinking's relation to creativity, and its susceptibility to development.

## Author's Note

I understand that this technique has been widely used in group work to facilitate creative attempts at problem solving. As far as I know, it has not been developed in ESOL. I do not know the exact origin of the technique.

*Christopher Sion*

# ANECDOTE ANALYSIS

**Unit II / CREATIVE WRITING AND THINKING / Level: Low intermediate and above /
Time: 30 minutes each, 2 days**

**Language Function(s):** Narrating; combining items of information

**Materials:** None

## In Class

1. Work with the class to create a story. The story can be based on anything: an amusing incident, something that has happened to the students in using their English, a few unrelated pictures, a book, or anything else. Encourage each student to make a contribution so that all the students can feel that it is their story. You may wish to write it on the board so that all the students can see it as it is constructed, or you may write it in a notebook as the students dictate it to you.

2. Before the next class, condense the story into about twelve sentences and type or print each sentence on a separate strip of paper. This is a good place to introduce new words: the students are likely to remember them because they are in "their" story. Make sure that the sentences include something from every member of the group and that there are enough strips so that each student will have one.

3. At the next session pass out the strips, making sure that everybody gets at least one. Then ask the class to put the story together in sequence. Provide help only if there is a serious problem.

4. Once the sentences are in the correct order, ask individual students to dictate the story to you and write it on the board. Hesitate obviously at garbled pronunciation and encourage the rest of the class to help in making you understand what to write. Allow time for those who want to copy the story for themselves.

5. There will probably be many verbs in the simple past, comparatives, and/or relative pronouns in the story. The exercise provides an opportunity to analyze and discuss these. Ask the students to tell you the words to write on the board for this purpose. You can also have them list regular past endings, put irregular verbs into their logical groupings, and cover other related points the class may have missed.

*Mike Perry*

**Unit II / CREATIVE WRITING AND THINKING / Level: Intermediate and above / Time: 30 minutes**

**Language Function(s):** Narrating; answering questions

**Materials:**    None

## Before Class

Prepare about ten comprehension questions similar to those used in standard comprehension tests. They can be based either on an existing passage from a textbook or on a passage that does not actually exist. Bring in whatever structures and vocabulary you wish to practice or reinforce. Up- or downgrade the questions to suit the level of the class. An example of a set of questions not based on a text but simply made up is as follows:

1. Why was David so exhausted when he got back to the village?

2. Was he surprised to find the village deserted? Why or why not?

3. The writer suggests three possible reasons why the village had been abandoned. Write two of them.

4. What did David discover on opening the front door of his cottage?

5. What would you have done in these circumstances? What did David do?

6. Which of the girls was real and which was a figment of David's imagination?

7. What led David to the realization that something was terribly wrong?

8. Do you think he was justified in being so violent? Why or why not?

9. How many survivors were discovered before dawn?

What was done with the remains of those who did not survive?

10. What would be a good title for the passage you have written?

## In Class

1. Review with the students the standard comprehension exercise technique in which they read a passage and then answer questions about it. If you have used exercises of this kind recently, you may wish to remind them of specific passages and questions. Tell them that they are going to do a variation of this technique this time. In fact, they are going to do such an exercise backwards.

2. Present the questions you have prepared to the students. You can either write them on the board or pass out duplicated copies of them. Tell the students that this time they are not to answer the questions but instead they are to write a passage on which the questions could be based. They are to be sure that every question will be able to be answered by reading the passage they write. (This allows the students to use their creative imagination within a framework set by you.)

3. When the passages have been completed, have them read aloud. You will probably find as many striking similarities as you will dissimilarities. Let the class discuss and compare the passages they have written.

4. Finally, if you have based your questions on a real passage, present this to the class either by reading it aloud, putting it on the board, or passing out duplicated copies. Discuss how the students' passages compare with the original. If you did not base your questions on an actual passage, this is the time to say so.

## Author's Note

I have found that there is sometimes a terrible anti-climax when the class is finally told that there isn't really a passage at all. It seems important not to actually lie to them when you present the instructions and questions.

*Jean-Paul Creton*

# WHAT SHOULD WE TALK ABOUT?

**Unit II / CREATIVE WRITING AND THINKING / Level: Low intermediate and above / Time: 40–50 minutes one day, 20–30 minutes second day**

**Language Function(s):** Exchanging ideas, reporting, narrating

**Materials:** None

## In Class

1. Start a discussion about what students are interested in. Then ask each student to write three topics in which he or she is interested on a piece of paper.

2. Divide the class into pairs, and ask each pair to discuss their lists and look for similarities. Then ask the pairs to join together to make groups of four. They should again discuss their lists. Circulate among the groups, noting popular topics.

3. Now ask a spokesperson for each group to tell the class the interests of that group. Following this, ask students, on the basis of these reports, to form new "interest-based" topic groups. Let them circulate freely and question others in order to find the group they want to join. You may end up with three or four definite interest groups. "Strays" should be urged to join one or another of the groups, whichever comes nearest to touching on their interests.

4. Tell the groups that they are to use the remainder of the period to prepare an introductory talk on their subject for a later class. Let the groups choose when they would like to give their talks, and arbitrate any schedule conflicts.

5. When the scheduled time comes, have the groups present their talks. Do not let one student dominate the proceedings, however; be sure that each one has the opportunity to speak. The discussion can continue with the whole class asking questions and making contributions and a student from any one of the groups taking the chair.

## Author's Note

Elements of this procedure can be adapted for use with students having differing needs in language improvement: the class can be divided into groups having similar difficulties.

*Chris Mills*

# UNIT 3

# READING AND WRITING

# III-1 HEADLINES

**Language Function(s):** Interpreting and suggesting

**Materials:** Newspaper articles; headlines from the articles cut into single words

## Before Class

Select newspaper articles with headlines appropriate to the level of your class. You will need about three articles for each of the small groups into which you will divide the class (Step 1). Cut the headlines off the articles and cut each headline into separate words. You may want to mount each article and each headline word on paper. This makes for easier handling and also ensures that students are seeing the correct side of the cut-out piece of newspaper and are not confused by what happens to be on the back. (For the purposes of the exercise it is preferable that all headlines be in the same type size and style.) Shuffle the words in the three headlines for each group and put them in envelopes so that all the words for the first group are in one envelope, those for the second group in another, and so on.

## In Class

1. Divide the class into small groups, and pass out the envelopes of shuffled headline words.

2. Tell the group that their envelopes contain words from three headlines. They are to reconstruct the headlines by putting the right words together. Tell them that you will provide the literal meaning of any words they don't understand but point out that headlines do not always use words in their literal sense: they must work out any metaphorical meanings for themselves.

3. Let the groups work for as long as necessary. Provide help where you think it is needed. Assembling the headlines should take about ten minutes, although this will vary with the level of the class.

4. When the headlines have been assembled, ask each group to read its headlines and tell what they mean and what the group feels the article was about. Then ask each student to take one of the headlines and write his or her own version of an article to go with that headline. (If there are more students than headlines, some can copy the headline and work from the copy.) The articles should be short, perhaps five to twelve sentences.

5. Then have the students read their articles to the class. Finally, they can compare their versions with the original articles from the newspaper. (You may need to edit the originals down to class level, but the exercise has more impact if they can at least see the original article in its printed form.)

*Chris Smith*

# DEAR ANN LANDERS

**Unit III / READING AND WRITING / Level: Intermediate / Time: 45 minutes**

**Language Function(s):** Discussing problems and solutions to problems; replying to letters

**Materials:** Letters and replies from typical, personal advice columns

## Before Class

Cut out several letters and their replies from typical advice columns such as "Dear Abby" or "Ann Landers." Paste them on cards, with a letter on one side of the card and the answer to a different letter on the other side. For example, the answer to letter "A" may appear on the back of letter "C," and so on. However the entire set will include all the letters and their answers.

## In Class

1. *Method One.* Have one student read one of the letters to the class. The class discusses the problem and suggests solutions. After one or more letters have been read and discussed, the students look at the backs of the cards for the columnist's answer and discuss that, comparing it with their own replies.

## Publisher's Note

*Method Two.* As an alternate, ask each student to write a reply to a letter that has been read to the class. Or give each student one of the letters and ask him or her to draft a reply to it. In either case, compare the student reply with the columnist's answer.

*Method Three.* (This can be used either as an alternative to Methods One and Two or as a follow-up to either.) Give each student a reply, and ask him or her to write a letter to which it might be the response. Then ask them to look through the cards and find the original letter. (If this Method is used as a follow-up, be sure that the responses used are not among those already seen by the class.)

2. After the students have completed the exercise with the letters, lead a discussion on related topics such as loneliness in the modern world, communication breakdowns between people, and what leads men and women to write to advice columns of this kind.

If your students are teenagers or young people in their early twenties, you may wish to use a column directed specifically toward young people. "Ask Beth" is one such syndicated column in the United States. However, both Abigail VanBuren ("Dear Abby") and Ann Landers include letters from young people as well as those from older adults, and their columns, because of wider syndication, may be easier to find.

*Mike Levy*

# III-3 HANDWRITING

**Language Function(s):** Speculating; describing; comparing

**Materials:** Two letters written in different scripts; pictures of people

## Before Class

Secure two handwritten letters, one of which is a reply to the other. The letters should be very different in style and written in very different scripts. The letters should be one or two pages in length so that they can easily be read by the students.

## In Class

1. Pass around the two letters. If you can make photo-duplicated copies, this will speed the exercise, but make sure that you also have the originals so that students see that these are real letters. Allow time for each student to read both letters.

2. Discuss the content of the letters and the background of the situation in which they were written. (If they were written "to order" for you, you will need to invent a plausible background for them.)

3. Now have the class describe the people who wrote the letters. Elicit a general personal description to-

gether with details of the writers' lifestyles. The different handwritings and the variations in literary style provide powerful stimuli for imagining what the writers are like.

4. Distribute magazine pictures of people to serve as additional (or alternative) stimuli, and ask the students, perhaps working in pairs, to say which two people the correspondence might have been between and to explain the reasons for their choices.

5. As a follow-up, have each student write a handwritten reply to the second letter. (This is a good exercise for homework, and you may wish to correct their letters as you would other homework exercises.) At the next session, return the letters to the students, divide the class into groups of four to six, and ask them to compare their styles of writing and their scripts. Do they have any memories of learning to write? Do their varying scripts say anything about themselves?

*Cynthia Beresford*

**Unit III / READING AND WRITING / Level: Intermediate and above / Time: 60 minutes**

**Language Function(s):** Sending and interpreting messages; writing letters; using the telephone

**Materials:** Telegram messages, one per student

## Before Class

Prepare a set of telegrams, one for each student. If possible, type these on yellow telegraph forms so that they approximate the appearance of a delivered telegram; in any case, each should be on a separate piece of paper, approximately telegram size and shape. Some examples of the kind of thing you might include are:

  a. YOUR HUSBAND INJURED. IN HOSPITAL HERE. ASKING FOR YOU. J. WHITE

  b. UNCLE BILL DIED TODAY. HEART ATTACK. CONDOLENCES. MARGARET

  c. PLEASE SEND MONEY. PASSPORT STOLEN. IN POLICE STATION. JOHN

  d. CONGRATULATIONS BILL AND LINDA. ALL HAPPINESS TO YOU. FREDA

  e. CANCEL TICKETS. LEG BROKEN. LETTER FOLLOWS. KEN

## In Class

1. Review with the class the form and use of telegrams as compared with those of letters and telephone messages, and give each student one of the telegrams you have prepared.

2. Divide the class into pairs. Working together, members of a pair decide what the relationship is between sender and recipient for each of the two telegrams. Then they choose one of the telegrams and write a letter to its recipient, expanding on the telegram's content.

3. The pair members then improvise a telephone conversation between sender and recipient of the other telegram.

4. Collect the letters, work with the students on errors, and then pass the letters around the class together with the telegrams on which they were based.

5. Have the improvised telephone conversations performed as dialogues. Before each dialogue, one member of the pair should read aloud the telegram on which the dialogue is based.

## Variations

a. Letters (Step 4) can be answered by other pairs or individual students.

b. Students can write telegrams themselves before writing letters or improvising conversations.

c. Students can be given a situation and then asked to write telegrams with a limited number of words. (Check with your local telegraph office for "full rate" limitations and limitations on other kinds of telegrams. Students might wish to convey the same information in a full-rate telegram and, for example, a night letter telegram.)

d. Students themselves can telephone the telegraph company and obtain information on rates and word limitations. They can also find out about overseas telegrams to different parts of the world. Under what conditions is the address counted as part of the message? The name of the sender? Can punctuation marks be used, and if so which marks? Are there any situations today in which the word "stop" must be used to signify the end of a sentence?

*Marjorie Baudains*

# EXTENSIVE READING

## Unit III / READING AND WRITING / Level: Advanced / Time: 40 minutes

**Language Function(s):** Extracting information from written texts; scanning; asking and answering questions

**Materials:** A newspaper

### Before Class

Prepare newspaper pages for each member of the class. Be sure that each page has two or more complete articles on it.

### In Class

1. Give one newspaper page to each member of the class.

2. Tell the students that they are to read one of the articles on their page, and then to write a question about that article on the board. They are not to identify the article on which the question is based. The question should be such that it can be answered only by reading the article. When they have written their question, they are to return the newspaper page to you.

3. Spread all the newspaper pages on the table in random order. Then ask the students to find the answers to the questions on the board. This will require quick, efficient reading of the material as they circulate, scanning the articles on the pages, then reading to find the answer to the question after they have located the proper article.

4. Go through the answers with the class as soon as the first person has finished. If you wish, you may discuss with the students the kind of reasoning they used to locate the correct articles.

*Paul Cammack*

**Unit III / READING AND WRITING / Level: Intermediate and above / Time: 60 minutes**

**Language Function(s):** Explaining and justifying choices; describing

**Materials:**   Old magazines

## In Class

1. Bring a pile of old magazines into class and tell the students to spend the next fifteen minutes leafing through them, looking especially at the advertisements.

2. Now tell the students to select some or all of the following:

   a. an advertisement they like

   b. an advertisement they hate

   c. an advertisement they think is a good one

   d. an advertisement they think is a bad one

3. Go around the class, asking each student to describe and discuss one of the advertisements he or she has chosen. The students should explain and justify their choices. Encourage questions and comments from the rest of the class.

4. Write on the board any advertising slogans, catch phrases, or other things you may wish to draw attention to; these items should flow out of points brought up in Step 3. Discuss these with the class, calling for examples from some of the selected ads.

*David Hill*

# AMBIGUITY IN ADVERTISING

**Unit III / READING AND WRITING / Level: Intermediate and above / Time: 45 minutes**

**Language Function(s):** Detecting ambiguity; interpreting figurative language; interpreting non-verbal graphic cues; recognizing connotative and denotative meanings

**Materials:** Magazines with advertisements or advertisements cut from magazines

## Before Class

Cut out and mount several advertisements containing slogans that have double meanings. For more advanced groups, bring in old magazines from which the students can select such ads.

## In Class

1. Pass out the advertisements to the group and analyze the double meanings in the slogans or headlines. (With more advanced groups you may have them locate such advertisements in old magazines. They can work in pairs, in small groups, or as a whole class.)

2. Discuss the reasons that advertisers use the language they do. Why, for example would an advertiser for jeans coin and use the phrase, "We've given your waist a little squeeze!"?

3. Ask the students to analyze other factors (apart from slogans) that advertisers use to catch the eye. For example, how are the subjects positioned? What is the layout like? How are the connotations (associated meanings) of words used in contrast to their denotations? What is the target audience of a particular ad? What social class, age, generation, or sex is being appealed to, and how does the student know this? How are stereotypes made use of? At which subconscious areas of the personality is the ad directed? How does the student know?

*Chris Mills*

**Language Function(s):** Appreciating syntax

**Materials:** Newspapers or magazines

## Before Class

Select pages from the newspapers or magazines which are suitable for your students.

## In Class

1. Give each student one of the pages you have selected. The pages need not be the same.

2. Ask the students each to select an article from their page—preferably something that interests them, and to pick one or two sentences from it. Any sentences will do, but the total number of words should not exceed twenty-five. Explain any unknown vocabulary to the students individually.

3. Ask the class to write their sentences in *vertical* columns of five words with adequate spacing between both the words and the columns. The students should write on pieces of paper, which you will later collect. For example, the sentences: "'We have other inquiries going on,' a police spokesman said. Early reports had said that police were looking for heroin and LSD." should be written:

| | | | | |
|---|---|---|---|---|
| WE | ON | EARLY | POLICE | AND |
| HAVE | A | REPORTS | WERE | LSD |
| OTHER | POLICE | HAD | LOOKING | |
| INQUIRIES | SPOKESMAN | SAID | FOR | |
| GOING | SAID | THAT | HEROIN | |

4. Collect the sheets of paper with the columns of words. Redistribute them making sure that no student receives his or her own sheet. Now ask the students to make new sentences using the columns of words. They should work *horizontally* and add words of their own as in the example below. The sentences may be any length but must be grammatically and syntactically correct.

WE *were* ON *the road*

HAVE *always given* A *look at our them*

OTHER *substances of interest to the* POLICE . *We*

INQUIRIES *about it. A* SPOKEMAN *for the police*

GOING *all over the country. He* SAID *also*

EARLY *but the* POLICE *noticed us* AND *stopped us. We*

REPORTS *which* WERE *about* LSD *and*

HAD *been* LOOKING *for heroin and making*

SAID *they had searched* FOR *years,*

THAT *they were sure* HEROIN *was being sold here.*

CAPITALS = the original sentences from the newspaper *Handwriting* = the student's contribution

*Marjorie Baudains*

# UNIT 4

# IV-1 GRAPHIC EXPERIENCES

**Language Function(s):** Identifying emotions

**Materials:** Cassette recorder; taped dialogue or short video sequence (in which case you will also need a video recorder and monitor)

## Before Class

Select a tape or video sequence of two people talking. The language should have strong emotional impact.

## In Class

1. Tell the class you are going to play them a short dialogue; you may wish to brief them on the content in a couple of sentences. Play the dialogue once. Ask the students to identify the characters: Who are they? What is their relationship? Where are they? Then ask the class to discuss what the characters are feeling and why. This is perhaps best done in pairs or small groups.

2. Tell the students that you are going to play the tape again and that their task is to draw a graph of what they hear. Ask them to take out a piece of paper and a pen and to draw two axes in preparation for the "graphic experience." Help by drawing on the board a horizontal and vertical axis similar to this:

```
        Angry |
              |
EMOTIONS      |
              |
        Calm  |_____
              PROGRESS of dialogue
```

Tell the students to draw in the graphs of *both* characters, perhaps using different colors. Warn them that they might not be able to keep up with the tape but that you will play it, several times if necessary, so they should just relax and include as much as they can. Then play the tape and allow the students to draw their graphs as described.

3. Divide the class into pairs again and ask the students to swap their graphs and explain what they have drawn. This should force them to recall the language used in the dialogue, for example: "This is where the woman screams that she can't go on."

4. Play the tape again, this time asking the students to write some of the key phrases on their graphs. This can be done in pairs or as an individual exercise. Don't hesitate to replay the tape if the class needs to hear it again. Then invite one student (or pair) to the front to draw his or her representation on the board and fill in the language at the key points. Discuss this with the class, inviting comparisons, or if necessary, corrections. When analyzing the language, pay particular attention to the intonation and register patterns found in the dialogue.

5. This can be followed up by giving the students a list of sentences for intonation practice. Some very productive examples are:

I'll always love you.      I'll do it tomorrow.

I don't think so.      I thought I left it here.

Do you really?

Ask the students to recite the sentences aloud with what they think is the correct intonation for whichever emotions are represented in the graph, for example anger, threat, or persuasion. Encourage the students to repeat their efforts several times. Finally, divide the class into pairs to simulate a situation where one or two of these sentences are used in a particular and deliberate functional way, for instance to express disagreement.

## Author's Note

I should like to acknowledge that step 5 draws heavily on Robert O'Neill's *Interaction* (Longman, London.)

*Jane Lockwood*

# **I**NNER LISTENING

**Unit IV / LISTENING / Level: Intermediate and above / Time: 30 minutes**

**Language Function(s):** Making associations; narrating; asking questions

**Materials:** Taped piece of music; cassette recorder

## Before Class

Choose a short piece of music which is without words and is appropriate to your group. You will either have to obtain a cassette version of it or be prepared to play it on the guitar, piano, or other instrument.

## In Class

1. Ask the class to listen to the music quietly as you play it for them once. Then ask the students to jot down all the thoughts, images, and feelings that go through their heads while you play the music a second time. Tell them to write freely, without bothering about grammar or organization.

2. Divide the class into pairs and let students choose what they want to relate to their partners from these notes. Then have the partners exchange their stories, anecdotes, feelings, and associations. They should listen closely and should be able to repeat their partner's account to the partner's satisfaction.

3. Ask *one student from each pair* to leave the room. The rest of the class should stay there. *Both groups* of students should select new partners. Using the first poem, they should recount the stories they have just heard to these new partners. In other words, they should retell their original partner's story as if it were their own.

4. Bring the class back together. Each person must find his or her original story by questioning the others, who relate the *second* story they were told. The exercise ends when discovery is complete. You may wish to round things off with a final playing of the music.

## Author's Note

This is a somewhat shorter version of my article "Inner Listening," which may be found in Spaventa et al. *Towards the Creative Teaching of English* (Heinemann).

*Lou Spaventa*

**Unit IV / LISTENING / Level: All / Time 20–30 minutes**

**Language Function(s):** Combining items of information

**Materials:** Taped song; copies of song written line for line on cardboard strips; cassette recorder

## Before Class

Select a song that relates to the level and interests of your class. It is not important if the class knows the music, but they should not be conversant with the lyrics, and the song should not be too long. Copy the words, line by line, onto thin cardboard; make enough copies so that there will be one for about every three students. Then cut up the cardboard so that each line of the song is on a separate strip. Shuffle the strips for each set.

## In Class

1. Divide the class into groups of three and distribute one of the cut-up cardboard sets to each group. Their task is to sort them into the correct order. New vocabulary can be pre-taught or explained as problems arise.

2. Play the song on the cassette; it should initially be *too soft to hear*. Keep on replaying it, gradually increasing the volume, but without attracting attention to yourself. The exercise works best when sorting out the lines proves a little too difficult for the group and the music becomes clearly audible just as the students' attention is beginning to wander. They suddenly realize that if they listen, they *can* find the words.

3. When the groups have all finished sorting the lines, collect the sets of strips so you can use them again. If possible, give the class a handout with the text or write it on the board (perhaps with the students dictating to you), and then let the class write it down so that they have a written record of the song. Then explain anything that is not altogether clear, answer questions, and finally sing the song with the group, perhaps allowing one of the students to take the lead.

4. One drawback is that this technique can only be used really effectively the first time it is done, as after that the element of surprise gets lost. If you want to use it again, try including several mistakes in the text. If the students are listening they'll pick them up. If they miss them you can prompt them, either generally ("Does that make sense to you?" "Everyone happy about that?") or in more detail ("Why do you think she says x in a song about y? Would you have said that?")

*Christopher Sion*

**Unit IV / LISTENING / Level: Intermediate / Time: 30–60 minutes**

**Language Function(s):** Narrating; describing; comparing

**Materials:** Suitable taped song, cassette recorder

## Before Class

Select the song you are going to use. I have chosen the "Unhappy Housewife" song from Abbs and Freebairn's *Strategies* (Longman, London). The song is recorded on *Skyhigh*, the accompanying tape. Other narrative songs could be used in the same way.

## In Class

1. Teach the class the song so that they know it thoroughly. Divide the class into pairs and ask them to tell about the song they heard. When they are finished, ask them to comment on what has happened and to discuss where they think the woman is going and what sort of reception she is going to have. (The song deals with a housewife who finally walks out on the man whose housework she has faithfully done down the years.) Ask the pairs to report back to the class.

2. Now ask the students to visualize the characters and describe them, their general background and way of life, hopes and fears, likes and dislikes, in as much detail as interest allows. A variation is to distribute aspects of the description among the class. One pair works on the description of the man, another on the woman, a third on their house, the family or the man's job, for example. Then the

students swap notes and try to reach agreement on a coherent class picture of the characters and their background.

3. Set up a role-play of the situation. This should include roles for friends and other members of the family, a marriage guidance counselor, perhaps even the milkman! But remember that this is dangerous territory and could prove extremely painful to a class member who has (or whose parents have) actually separated. You might continue by switching the students around and letting them play several different roles, but do not allow the activity to become boring by going on too long.

4. Step 3 can lead on to the discussion of the roles of men and women, wives and husbands, or of cultural differences and role definitions. Another follow-up exercise is for students to write a further verse for the song, or even a new song giving the husband's point of view. Or the students could make up letters from estranged couples to practice a wide range of different styles; for example heartbroken, threatening, cold, formal, pre-divorce, or wanting to make up. If interest permits, the students could finally be asked to reply to one of the others' letters.

## Author's Note

It goes without saying that not *all* these ideas should always be used. Try discussing them with your class and letting them decide what they want to do.

*David Sanders*

## Editor's Note

This recipe deals specifically with one particular song. Other songs could be used in a similar way by adapting the instructions to the content.

**Language Function(s):** Asking questions

**Materials:** None

The key to this activity lies in using the students' initials to generate vocabulary. It is therefore imperative that everyone knows each others' names. You also need to be sure you have enough ideas for those with less common initials to keep the pace moving.

## In Class

### Method One

1. Explain to the group that the class is going on an imaginary expedition. The students must try to establish what they may take with them by asking questions. For example: "May I take my shoes?" "Can Mary take her cigarettes?" Ask the students to write down a few questions to get them going. Once the exercise is underway there should be plenty of spontaneous questions for them to ask.

2. Answer simply "Yes" or "No" according to the following system: *Roberto* can take a *rifle*, a *rug*, some *rice*—anything that begins with the letter "r" as his name does. Similarly, *Cathy* can take *cake*, *cola*, *cornflakes* and so on, but not root beer, asparagus or bananas.

3. Encourage the class to dredge up as many words as they can so as to yield a lot of vocabulary. The students who manage to grasp the system should *not* tell the others. Instead, get them to take over your role in answering the questions.

### Editor's Note

No prizes for decoding the title!

### Method Two

This is a more complex version which is based on both initials and can be used to practice the passive. Begin with yourself and your "ship." A sentence based on *Mike Lavery* might be: "My ship is powered by *m*armalade and sinks with *l*emonade." Go on to single out the students, saying to *Alberto Bender*, for example: "Alberto, your ship is powered by *a*pples and sinks with *b*ottles." The students may ask questions to try and find out about their own (and their classmates') ships. They should not let on if they crack the code, but should simply join in, making statements about themselves and the others. This allows you to fade into the background gradually until total student-student interaction has been established. Only intervene if there is a lapse in the exchanges.

If you want to bring in a still more complicated dimension, base the vocabulary on the initials of the person sitting on a given person's left or right.

*Mike Lavery and Ian Butcher*

# SOUNDS DIFFERENT

**Unit IV / LISTENING / Level: Intermediate / Time: 20–30 minutes**

**Language Function(s):** Identifying and practicing sounds

**Materials:** Cards with an illustration on one side and, ideally, the relevant word written on the other, with contrasts such as "bear/beer" or "pen/pan." Ann Baker's *Ship and Sheep: Introducing English Pronunciation* (Cambridge University Press) has some excellent examples.

## Before Class

Select the pairs of pictures you want to use.

## In Class

1. Show the class the pictures one by one and ask the students to identify the objects in them. Elicit the vocabulary from the group as much as possible, prompting as necessary. Write the words in two numbered columns on the board on the basis of contrasting sounds, like this:

| 1 | 2 |
|---|---|
| beer | bear |
| pan | pen |
| bed | bad |
| | ETC. |

2. Say one of the words without indicating how it is spelled. The students have to decide which column on the board it comes from and should repeat the word. If they get the wrong column they must repeat *both* parts of the minimal pair, for example "ship/sheep."

3. Ask the students to call out words from the columns while the teacher or other students indicate which words they think are being said. Again, if the word has not been pronounced correctly, both parts of the minimal pair must be repeated.

4. Variations

   a. Give a sentence incorporating one of the relevant words and have the students choose which is correct, for example: "Yesterday I went for a ride in a ship" or "I had a beer with my dinner." Ask the class to make sentences in the same way.

   b. Put some of the cards in various places around the class and ask questions like "Where is the bear?" or "Is the pan on the table?"

   c. Divide the class into teams. Divide the cards equally between the teams and tell them to write a short story containing all the words on their cards*. When they are ready, a group spokesman reads the story to the rest of the class. Illustrate it on the board, pretending to misunderstand words that are incorrectly pronounced, so that the students have to emphasize. For example: "No, not ship; *sheep*." This will show that they have genuinely grasped the difference.

## *Author's Note

Be sure to check that the stories are in correct English. This can give you valuable insight into many other areas that need to be dealt with as a basis for future work.

*Mike Levy*

# EXTENSIVE/INTENSIVE LISTENING

**Language Function(s):** Asking and answering factual questions

**Materials:** Two recorded copies of a short news item or similar material; two cassette recorders; if possible, two rooms

## Before Class

Record something from the radio, for example an interesting news item, which is not too long but is at a level challenging to the class. Transfer it onto another tape so that you have two copies.

## In Class

1. Divide the class into two groups. If possible, arrange to have the groups in separate rooms. Give each group a tape recorder and a copy of the tape. Tell them to listen to the tape and then prepare questions about the material for the other group. Set a time limit. Circulate, keeping an eye on what the students are doing, but letting them organize themselves as much as possible.

2. The students re-assemble as one class. The groups should ask each other their questions while a "secretary" for each group writes down the answers. It is probably best to start by having each group ask one question of the other group so that the students from both groups are discussing their answers simultaneously. This working "in parallel" is most effective and is not difficult to organize. Make sure that students take turns at asking the questions; do not let one or two of them monopolize the activity.

3. Finally, replay the tape to the whole class. The students should check to be sure that their answers are correct. Draw attention to any inaccuracies they might have overlooked.

## Editor's Note

Don't be put off if two rooms aren't available for your class. Why not collaborate with another teacher? In this case each of the two classes would be one of the two groups.

*Frances Krish*

# AURAL COMPREHENSION IV-8

**Language Function(s):** Notetaking

**Materials:**   Short taped text or dialogue; cassette recorder

## Before Class

Choose a fairly short taped text suitable to the needs and interests of your class.

## In Class

1. Tell the students in one or two sentences what the tape is about and then play it through once. Do not tell the class to look for any particular elements.

2. Tell the group that you are going to play the tape again and that this time they should take notes when they hear it. Give them a minute or two to get out their writing materials and then play the tape through again from beginning to end without stopping, even if there are questions.

3. Divide the class into groups of three or four students. Their task is to compare their notes and discuss what they think the main points of the text were. Ask each group to elect a "secretary" to make a written summary. Circulate, answering any ques-

tions, helping as necessary, and making sure that the interaction is in English.

4. Ask each group to elect a representative to read, or if possible tell the class without reading verbatim, what they have written. The rest of the class should listen carefully and draw attention to any errors in the content or the language, perhaps by tapping on the desk with a pencil, or shouting out "Stop!" or "Challenge!"

5. While this is going on, write on the board (drawing as little attention to yourself as you can so as not to interrupt) any factually or grammatically incorrect sentences the students have overlooked. When the groups have all given their accounts, the students' attention should be turned to the material on the board and the class should be asked to correct the error without your help wherever possible. Finish off with a final playing of the text.

*Sonia Taylor*

**Language Function(s):** Notetaking

**Materials:** Story about two pages long

## Before Class

Find a story about two pages long. (Gattegno's *Short Passages* [Educational Solutions, New York City] contains ideal examples.) Pick out one or two long sentences that are of central importance in the story but do not occur at the beginning.

## In Class

1. Tell the class you are going to read them a sentence (or two) but *not* where it comes from or why. Ask the students to write down as many words and phrases as they can remember. Warn them that you will read the sentence(s) only *once*.

2. Read the sentence and then ask the students, working individually, to try to reconstruct it. If the students appear to find the task too difficult, read the sentence a second time. Then have the students continue their attempts at reconstruction. After they can make no further progress alone, suggest that they try working in pairs.

3. After a few minutes, tell the students to change partners. Let them move freely around the room, comparing sentences. When the class is fairly near the "solution," but are perhaps beginning to feel discouraged tell them to sit down and put their books away.

4. Start reading the story that the sentence was taken from as if this were a completely new activity. The class will gradually realize that the sentence they worked on comes from the story. When you have finished, let the students resume the reconstruction activity. Ask them to write the sentence on the board, working together as a group. With large classes you might need two parallel groups.

5. Finish by holding a discussion of the activity and the story with the whole class. What did they find most challenging? In the notetaking, were they distracted by trying to transcribe the material word for word? Or did they concentrate on picking out the main points? What *were* the main points?

*John Overton*

# ARE YOU SITTING COMFORTABLY?

Unit IV / LISTENING / Level: Low intermediate and above / Time: 20−40 minutes

**Language Function(s):** Narrating; comparing

**Materials:** None

## Before Class

Prepare the story by reading it quietly to yourself and then going through it several times aloud so that it will be "alive" when you come to present it to the class.

## In Class

1. Teach any unknown vocabulary and set the mood for the story: quiet calm and comfortable.

2. Read the story. You will find the text at the end of these instructions. Use any pauses or simple dramatic gestures for effect. Make sure you look up from the book. It will be far more difficult to hold the group's attention if you bury your head in the pages.

3. As the story is unfinished, ask the students in groups or pairs to write their own endings to it. Most students seem to want happy or trick endings such as: "The princess bribed the lionkeeper to feed the lion up so that it wasn't hungry," or "The King saw it as a sign from God when the lion turned away." Others may prefer a more twisted ending: "He fought the lion, won the fight, and then married the other woman anyway!" Circulate, helping the students express their ideas in writing.

4. When the groups have finished their versions, read or let a student read: ". . . acting on the decision she had made after days and nights of weighing the awful choice, she nodded to the right. The young man saw and without hesitating walked to the right-hand door and opened it." The groups then read their versions in turn, and share their feelings about them.

5. This may lead to further discussion about *why* they wanted their particular end to the story; what kinds of stories they liked as children, or the fascination of ghost stories and fairy stories. Moreover, some students will probably have some stories they would like to tell or favorite characters they want to describe.

### The Story

Many years ago in a country in North Africa there lived a king who had some very strange customs. One of these was the way he decided if a prisoner was guilty or not guilty. Whenever one of his subjects was accused of a serious crime, the king decided that the fate of the accused would be determined in front of the people. On the chosen day, the king, his followers, and all the people gathered on a small hill. In front of the hill was a big building with two doors, exactly alike, set side by side. At the king's signal, the accused would walk to the doors, and open one of them. Behind one door was a hungry lion which would eat the prisoner as a punishment for his crime. Behind the other door was a beautiful woman to whom the prisoner would be married immediately as a reward for his innocence.

The plan seemed most fair to the king. The accused could choose his own fate. He simply opened a door and was at once either eaten or married.

Now it happened that the king's beautiful daughter, whom he loved above all things, had fallen in love with a poor but handsome young soldier. When the king found out that they loved each other, he put the young man into prison and set a day for his public trial. Then the king ordered the whole kingdom to be searched for the biggest lion and the most beautiful woman.

Finally, the day of the trial arrived. The young man entered the field. He was so handsome that the crowd greeted him with a hum of admiration and fear. How terrible this was for him! Advancing into the field the handsome young soldier turned, as was his custom, and bowed to the king. But he fixed his eyes on the princess, who was sitting on her father's right. The young man saw in her eyes that the princess knew on which side the lion was and which the lady. There was not a moment to lose. His eyes asked her, "Which door shall I choose?"

The princess knew that the woman her father had chosen was the loveliest in the land. In the past she had seen this woman throw admiring glances at the soldier. Somtimes she even suspected that these glances were returned. How could she bear to lose her lover to another woman? How could she bear to see him torn apart by the lion? The princess paused. Then acting on the decision she had made after days and nights of weighing the awful choice, she nodded to the right. The young man saw, and without hesitating, walked to the right-hand door and opened it . . . . . . .

## Author's Note

This is an adaptation of the well-known story, "The Lady and the Tiger," by Frank R. Stockton. I first came across it in an examination set by the Ministry of Education of the United Republic of Tanzania.

*Mo Strangeman*

# MULTIPLE CHINESE WHISPERS    IV-11

**Unit IV / LISTENING / Level: Intermediate / Time: 45 minutes**

**Language Function(s):** Narrating; expressing disagreement

**Materials:**    Copies of the stories cited at the end of this recipe

## Before Class

Copy the texts following these instructions. Cut one copy into the individual stories.

## In Class

1. Have the students sit in a circle and give each of them one of the short stories from page 52. Tell the students to memorize the stories. Circulate, explaining vocabulary as necessary. Collect the stories so that you can use them again.

2. Ask every second student to turn to his or her left-hand neighbor and tell each other the stories they have memorized. If you have an odd number of students, join in yourself to make up an even number. After the students have finished, tell them to each turn to their *other* neighbor and tell the story they have just been told (*not* their original stories.) The students exchange their stories. Then, once

again, they turn back to their (left-hand) neighbors and repeat the stories they have just been told by their other (right-hand) neighbors. The exercise can continue either until all the stories have been passed right round the group or the students start showing signs of boredom.

3. Ask each student to tell the group the last story he or she has heard. This is unlikely to bear much resemblance to the original, and students can become quite argumentative about exactly what was told to them. This final stage is a useful functional exercise for expressing disagreement. (The first stage is a good structural exercise for practicing the narrative past simple.) Finish by handing out copies of the stories so the class has a written record of the material.

*Randal Holme*

The following are some sample stories. They are varied, and some of them are useful for promoting discussion about their meaning. Two have been intentionally selected because they are similar. Their use is particularly productive because the ensuing confusion produces genuine disagreement.

1. Once there was a head. The head saw so much that it wanted to be glass. The head saw everything. The head could not contain all it saw. The head burst into thousands of pieces. The pieces of glass became stars.

2. The king wanted to build a magnificent church. He found a builder. He said: "Build a church." The king was impatient. The builder finished the foundations and then he disappeared. The king was angry but he could do nothing. After ten years the builder came back. The king wanted to kill him. The builder said, "The foundations are ready. Now I can finish the church."

3. The king asked for a man to build an arch. The king wanted an arch to pass through. A builder built the arch. When it was finished the king passed under it. The arch was too low and knocked the king's crown off his head. The king said to the builder: "I will hang you." The builder said, "Hang the arch". When the king hanged the arch, he raised it . . .

4. The farmer liked to ride round his land on a donkey. Then he bought more land so he had to buy a horse. Then he bought more land so he had to buy a tractor. Soon he had so much land he had to buy a helicopter to go from end to end in a day. The helicopter was too fast. It took him over his land so quickly he thought the land was no longer his. He wanted to be large enough to eat all that his land produced. No man could be so large. He finally died of hunger.

5. The students asked their teacher: "What is the way?" The teacher did not answer. He only raised one finger. The next day, the teacher asked his students, "What is the way?" One student said, "The way is difficult," another said, "It is long," another said, "It is beautiful." "No, no!" the teacher said. He became angry. Then a student raised his finger. The teacher took a knife and cut the finger off. "That," he said, "is the way."

6. The Spanish fireman went to the fire. The fire was very dangerous. A woman was in the building. She could not leave. The Spanish fireman found a blanket. He called to the woman. He said, "Jump into my blanket!" The woman was afraid. The fire grew more dangerous. The woman jumped. She fell towards the blanket. Just before she reached the blanket, the fireman waved the blanket away and said: "Olé!"

7. The Captain left England in 1786. He sailed into the Pacific. He went further and further south. He saw a ship without sails moving towards him. He sailed away. When he returned to England he did not recognize it.

8. A ship was sailing from London to New York. The captain saw another ship. He called to it. He heard no answer. He went close. He went onto the ship. He found everything on the ship in order. There was no sign of violence. He took the ship back to London.

9. There was a country where men did not make art like nature, but nature unlike art. One day an artist made a rock look like a head when before everyone had made rocks look unlike heads. The King of the country was very pleased. He said: "Now the rock looks like me." A wise man said: "That head is better than your head! Now you must understand that as you are small and feeling small, you will act small; you will be like a beast."

10. A man bought a bottle. He opened the bottle and a genie flew out. The genie said: "What do you want?" The man wanted many things. The genie delivered them all. The man was surrounded by so many things that he could not climb over them. He was in prison.

**Language Function(s):** Sharing and summarizing information

**Materials:** Copies of the sentences at the end of this recipe

## Before Class

Copy the sentences on page 54 so that you have enough for all the members of your class. Cut one copy into strips with one sentence on each strip.

## In Class

1. Deal the eighteen sentences out among the group. If you have fewer than eighteen students it does not matter if some receive more than one strip. If you have a couple more than eighteen, let two students share one piece of information. Larger classes should be divided into two or even three groups.

2. Ask the students to keep their strips secret from the others. Their task is to memorize *the information* (not the actual sentences) on the strips. They should not learn the material "parrot fashion." Do not allow writing. Explain the vocabulary as necessary. Collect the strips so that you can use them again.

3. Ask the students to move about and share the information they have. Give minimal instructions. Allow enough time for the information to be shared thoroughly but do not let it go on the the point where the students become bored.

4. Ask the class to return to their seats. Their task is to write a summary of the information they have gathered. They may work individually or in pairs.

5. When they have finished, the students should compare notes with other pairs or individuals. Next, working as one group with a "secretary," they should produce a final version on the board. Then, if requested, you may give out copies of the original text for comparison.

*John Morgan*

## IV-12 PARALLELS (continued)

PARALLELS

| | |
|---|---|
| John F. Kennedy was murdered on a Friday. | Abraham Lincoln was murdered on a Friday. |
| John F. Kennedy was shot in the head by Lee Harvey Oswald. | Abraham Lincoln was shot in the head by John Wilkes Booth. |
| After the death of Abraham Lincoln, Andrew Johnson, the Vice-President, became President of the U.S.A. | After the death of John F. Kennedy, Lyndon Johnson, the Vice-President, became President of the U.S.A. |
| John Wilkes Booth was born in 1839. | Lee Harvey Oswald was born in 1939. |
| Booth shot Lincoln in a theater and then ran into a shop. | Oswald shot Kennedy from a shop and then ran into a theater. |
| John F. Kennedy had a secretary called Lincoln. | Abraham Lincoln had a secretary called Kennedy. |
| Andrew Johnson was born in 1808. | Lyndon Johnson was born in 1908. |
| Abraham Lincoln's wife was a brunette who spoke fluent French: she was 24 when she married Lincoln. | John F. Kennedy's wife was a brunette who spoke fluent French: she was 24 when she married Kennedy. |
| John F. Kennedy's father, Joseph, was Ambassador to London. | Abraham Lincoln's son, Robert, was Ambassador to London. |

# UNIT 5

# ROLE PLAYING

# V-1 STUDENTS FOR SALE

**Language Function(s):** Giving information; persuading

**Materials:**   Advertising slogans

## Before Class

Cut out some advertisements from magazines or newspapers taking care to choose items that should appeal to your class. If you can't find any, think up a few imaginary advertising slogans and details of non-existent products and special offers.

## In Class

1. Bring the materials you have gathered into class and use them to "brainstorm" advertising slogans. This will warm the group up in preparation for the second part of the activity.

2. Divide the class into pairs. One person in each pair is A, the other is B. Tell both the A's and B's to think of a product they would each like to be. Once this has been decided, move into the marketing phase. A is the marketing person for B, and B the market-ing person for A. A must prepare a promotional advertising "spiel" for B, who meanwhile does the same for A. A and B should consult each other about what they should say. Lying and exaggerating are to be encouraged. Walk around the class, supplying vocabulary, helping with ideas if necessary, and correcting mistakes.

3. When the class is ready, each student presents his or her "product" to the group and gives the promotional spiel. The product should try to demonstrate some of the talents attributed to him or her wherever possible. For example the marketing person says she can speak French and the product says "Oui!" The promotion should be similar to a TV commercial, with a commentator and some visual action.

*Nancy Osmond*

# CREATING IDENTITIES: An Input Activity

## Unit V / ROLE PLAYING / Level: Intermediate and above / Time: 60 minutes

**Language Function(s):** Exchanging and comparing personal information; narrating

**Materials:** Cards with key phrases as described in step 4; a large room with furniture that can be moved around easily

### Before Class

Write the key phrases on the cards as described in step 4.

### In Class

1. Tell the class to divide themselves into three families or groups of people living together. Each family or group should make its own area, if possible using chairs, tables, boxes, and whatever else is available.

2. Ask the students to work out identities for themselves in their groups and to establish their relationships to one another. Ask them to build up their characters, referring to daily habits, deciding who are the breadwinners, and so on. Stay in the background but provide help with vocabulary and structures as necessary. Try to let the identities come from the students themselves as much as possible.

3. Ask the three groups, (who should remain in their areas) to face each other. Then tell them they should introduce themselves to the class.

4. Next, tell the groups to imagine that they all know each other. They should move around and establish among themselves when, where, and how they met. Introduce the past tense as required*. Use key phrases such as: "We met when we were in . . . ,"

"I first saw you . . . ," or "We went to . . ." written on cards which are passed to the students who need them.

5. Send the students "home" to their original areas and tell them it is, for example, early Friday evening and that they should act out what they would be doing in their assumed roles. Encourage them to move around, visiting each other's homes or going out.

6. After a few minutes shout out, for example: "It is now 10 P.M. What are you doing now?" and then after a further few minutes: "It is now 1 A.M.," and so on. Continue in this way through Saturday and Sunday. In each case the characters should act out what they would be doing at the time given.

7. Finally, establish that it is Monday evening. Ask the students to gather around and face each other again. Use the material just generated to practice questions and answers in the past tense:
   —Where did you on Saturday night?—I went to a concert.
   —Did you meet Lucy?—No, I didn't. I stayed at home.
   —Why didn't you go out on Sunday afternoon?—Because my mother came over for lunch.

### *Author's Note

I use this activity primarily to *input* new structural material. However, such exercises can also be used as follow-up material for more advanced students. Moreover, this kind of exercise is neither limited to the past tense, nor to the concept of families. It could be adapted to the future, or set in a business context where the groups have to form corporations, agree about what they are trading, and then trade.

*John Overton*

# AN IMPROVISED ROLE PLAY

V-3

**Language Function(s):** Asking and answering questions

**Materials:** None

## In Class

1. "Brainstorm" on the board a concept or an object which will yield a rich collection of adjectives, for example, "the sea," which might produce words such as cool, calm, rough, unpredictable, blue, wet, stormy, beautiful and so on. Other good words to start with are "space" and "garden."

2. Ask the class which of the adjectives on the board could be applied to a person. Then ask the students to *imagine* an individual to whom all these words could apply, and to spend a couple of minutes thinking about what sort of person he or she would be. Build up a quick, superficial outline of this character by asking questions like: "Is it a man or a woman? How old is he or she? What does he or she do for a living? What is his or her social background?" Do not dwell on the discussion at this stage: accept the first, spontaneous replies from the class.

3. Invite one student to assume the role of the character that has been suggested. Tell the others that this person is about to join them as a colleague at their place of work. Ask them to question this individual closely to find out whether they will be happy to accept this character as a workmate. Is he or she the sort of person they think they could get along with? The role player must develop the character but adhere as strictly as possible to the framework of the original adjectives applied to this particular individual. This will almost certainly involve their trying to work out any apparent contradictions in the group of adjectives.

4. When the students are confident they have an assessment of the role player's personality, the others should each give a personal view of the character portrayed. The role player should also join in the discussion on his or her character, retaining the role. Did the group correctly interpret the personality from the character's own point of view? It is a particularly rewarding exercise if you manage to finish by arriving at a consensus.

*Richard Baudains*

# THE OPEN-ENDED INTERVIEW

## Unit V / ROLE PLAYING / Level: Low intermediate and above / Time: 5–20 minutes

**Language Function(s):** Asking and answering questions

**Materials:**    None

### Before Class

Select one or more characters from any story, dialogue, book, or picture that the class has recently studied. It should be a fictional, not a real-life person. Prepare questions to ask as described below.

### In Class

1. Assign the role(s) of the character(s) to one (or more) of your better students. Tell them to respond to the questions you will ask them. Suppose the class has studied Poe's story "Cask of Amontillado." Announce that students X and Y are to be Montressor and Fortunato. Immediately begin by firing "nosey-reporter" questions at them.* These should be questions that do not have answers in the story. Simply invent the questions as you go along once you have used all your prepared questions.

Example:

Teacher:    Fortunato, are you married?

Student X: Yes.

Teacher:    What did your wife do when you failed to come home after visiting Montressor?

Student X: Well, you see, she was having an affair with him and she knew about the plot all along.

Teacher:    Montressor, is that true?

And so on.

2. Once the students are familiar with the game, let the class members themselves assume the roles of reporters interviewing the others. Finish with a discussion of how convincing the characters' accounts are. How would the other students have responded to the questions?

### *Author's Note

The teacher rather than a student acts as interviewer *at first*, to ensure that the questions will be far-ranging and unexpected, and to guide the students away from looking for answers anywhere but in their imaginations. By holding such interviews frequently, all the students will eventually have the chance to be on the "firing line."

*John Pint*

# LITTLE JOHNNY'S ACCIDENT

## V-5

**Unit V / ROLE PLAYING / Level: Intermediate / Time: 60 minutes**

**Language Function(s):** Narrating; justifying; answering questions

**Materials:** Overhead projector; transparency copy of the figures on page 61

### Before Class

Copy the figures on page 61 onto one overhead projector transparency. Cut out the squares with the figures of the characters, the stop sign, silhouette of the truck, etc.

### In Class

1. Place the transparency showing the road on the projector. Move the cut-out of little Johnny riding his bicycle and tell the following story, laying the other cut-outs in the appropriate places at the appropriate times to illustrate the incident.

   "One day last week little Johnny was riding his bicycle along a narrow country lane. He wasn't paying attention because he was thinking about his dinner, so when he came to the stop sign he didn't stop. He went straight into the road. A truck was coming around the corner, and because the driver didn't see Johnny, he didn't stop. The truck crashed into Johnny and knocked him down. Mrs. Brown was waiting at the bus stop on the corner and she saw the accident. Mr. Smith was driving his car in the other direction, and he saw the accident, too."

2. Ask one of the students to come to the front and move the cut-outs around and retell the story while the class corrects him or her on points of fact and grammar. (Do not spend more than about five minutes on this.)

3. This step involves setting up a role play based on the accident. Assign the roles of Johnny, Mrs. Brown, Mr. Smith and the truck driver; the remaining students play the parts of police officers. Depending on numbers, you may have to set up two parallel role plays. Send each of the witnesses to a different part of the room and tell the police to go and interview them. Each officer should speak to at least two witnesses and they should take down written reports of the accident. Tell Johnny and Mrs. Brown (privately) to insist that Johnny was *not* responsible. They should say, for example, that he *did* stop, the truck driver was drunk, Mr. Smith is nearsighted, and so on.

4. Bring the main characters and the police officers together in a courtroom scene. In a big class where you have had to work with more than one group you will need to set up two such scenes. The police make their reports and everybody tries to convince the judge (played either by the teacher or ideally by an outsider who knows nothing about the accident) that their version is correct. This usually involves a great deal of genuine disagreement because of the variety of different accounts. In this way the activity closely mirrors the problems that arise in everyday life when several witnesses to an incident all perceive it differently. You might like to round the lesson off with a discussion of this topic.

*Jim Brims*

**61**

#  THE COURTROOM ROLE PLAY

**Unit V / ROLE PLAYING / Level: Intermediate and above / Time: 60−90 minutes (depending on inclusion of step 3)**

**Language Function(s):** Making and justifying decisions

**Materials:** Copies of the three court cases on page 63; copies of possible sentences.

## Before Class

Make enough copies of the cases to go round the class.

## In Class

1. Divide the class into groups of three or four. Give each group one case from those to be found on the following page and allow them 15 minutes to reach a verdict and pass sentences. Circulate, helping with vocabulary and points of information (e.g. in Case 2, giving details of how much a family might get on welfare) but *not* with ideas. Give each group also a copy of the possible sentences. Tell students to follow this range in passing sentences.

2. Where time and interest allow, you may wish to have each group try each case. When the groups have reached their decisions, let a student be appointed in each group to read out the verdicts, which you should write on the board in chart form so that they may be compared easily. Write the possible penalties in one column down the side and then add one column for each group's verdicts for each of the three cases. Make sure that reasons are given for the decisions. Finish off by inviting an open discussion of the various group verdicts.

3. The groups might then like to make up a case of their own, either suggesting a sentence, or offering it to another group to try, or both. Again, the verdicts should be written on the board as described in step 2 and the lesson rounded off with a comparison of the verdicts and the groups' justifications.

*David Hill*

## YOU ARE THE MAGISTRATES ON THE BENCH OF A MAGISTRATES' COURT

*Case 1*

A man of 50 comes before you, accused of breaking into a hardware store and stealing woodworking tools worth $150. He pleads guilty.
You must reach a verdict and pass sentence.

*Points to consider:*

1. He was a carpenter for 30 years with one company and was recently laid off.

2. He has been unemployed for six months.

3. He says that his only hope of finding work is to have his own set of tools.

4. It is his first offense.

Discuss this and come to a decision. What sentence would you pass? And why?

## YOU ARE THE MAGISTRATES ON THE BENCH OF A MAGISTRATES' COURT

*Case 2*

A woman comes before you accused of shoplifting from Sears'. The police say she took two tea towels and six glasses (total value $6.50.)
She pleads not guilty.
You must read a verdict and pass sentence.

*Points to consider:*

1. It is her first offense.

2. Her husband has been unemployed for one year.

3. She has six children.

4. She has lived in America for two years but she can't speak English.

5. She says (through an interpreter) that she did not know that she had to pay, as the system is different in her country.

Discuss this and come to a decision. What sentence would you pass? And why?

## YOU ARE THE MAGISTRATES ON THE BENCH OF A MAGISTRATES' COURT

*Case 3*

A boy of 14 comes before you accused of setting his school on fire. This caused $5000 worth of damage. He pleads guilty.
You must reach a verdict and pass sentence.

*Points to consider:*

1. He lives with his mother and four younger brothers and sisters.

2. His father died two years ago.

3. His mother works in a store during the day and in a bar in the evening to get enough money.

4. His school grades are terrible and he is constantly in trouble for playing hooky, fighting and breaking rules.

5. It is not his first offense. A year ago he was accused of stealing $25 from the drugstore where he had a Saturday job. He was let go with a warning.

Discuss this and come to a decision. What sentence would you pass? And why?

Possible Sentences, Cases 1, 2, 3

Fine ($1000 maximum)
Imprisonment (six months maximum)
Community service
Placement in a foster home (persons under age 16)
Placement in a reform school or similar facility (persons under 16)
Probation
Acquittal

# V-7 POLITICAL CAMPAIGNS

**Language Function(s):** discussing and presenting promises and intentions

**Materials:**   None

## In Class

1. Discuss with the class the form of a typical election manifesto or platform statement and the language used in such statements. Build up a short list of examples on the board like this:

| My party is going to | −increase public spending |
|---|---|
| We intend to | −reintroduce the draft |
| Our plan is to | −reduce taxation |
| We promise to | −legalize drugs |

(One possible starting point is the examples in *Starting Strategies* By Brian Abbs and Ingrid Fairbairn, published by Longman.)

2. Divide the class into threes or fours, and tell each group to decide on a political party they would like to belong to. The optimum number is three groups but this will obviously to some extent depend on the size of the class. Encourage the students to innovate—they need not follow established party lines. Tell them to be as imaginative as they like. A few suggestions might be a drivers', cyclists', or pedestrians' party; one for men's, women's, or children's liberation; or one dedicated to American or European unification.

3. Ask each group to prepare an election platform and to elect one member to present the party program to the rest of the class. Circulate, helping as necessary and correcting the language.

4. Have the party representatives make their speeches, one by one. Encourage questions and even heckling while they are speaking. Further questioning can take place once the speech is over, when any members of the party may be called on to reply.

5. Finish with a mock election including a vote by secret ballot. Depending on the group, this could in turn provoke discussion of any recent political incidents, or of a related topic such as comparative electoral systems or procedures, or even of the philosophy and principles underlying democracy.

*Sonia Taylor*

# UNIT 6

# STRUCTURES AND FUNCTIONS

# VI-1 INTRODUCTIONS

Unit VI / STRUCTURES AND FUNCTIONS / Level: Low intermediate to Intermediate /
Time: 45 minutes

**Language Function(s):** Introducing; interrupting

**Materials:** Labels or name tags

## In Class

1. Discuss different forms of etiquette and rituals of meeting people and compare them with the American forms. Who is introduced to whom? (Consider such variables as age, sex, status and so on. What do you say when you are introduced? Must you stand up?) Let the class initiate the forms of introduction as much as possible. Some basic examples might be:

   —Could/Can/May I introduce you to . . . . . . . . . .

   —Let me introduce you to . . . . . . . . . . .

   —Have you guys met before? Karl, this is Claudia.

   —This is (my friend/my sister) Lisa.

   —George—Agnes. (Agnes—George.)

   —Sally, do you know, have you met . . . . . . . . .

   Some examples of conversational gambits that may be used in maneuvering one guest away from another, are:

   —Can I interrupt/break in . . . . . . . . . . ?

   —Do you mind if I take her away/borrow her for a moment?

   —Can you spare him for a moment?

   —You (simply) must meet . . . . . . . . . . .

   —There's someone I'm just dying for you to meet!

   Consider any other examples you might want to use in reference to age, sex, social status and environment. Discuss any experiences the students might have have had.

2. Divide the class into threes. Each student takes a turn at being the host or hostess and practices some of the language forms that have been looked at above.

3. Give the students labels or name tags. Ask each student to think of one well-known or imaginary person and one piece of information about this person, and write the name and information on the label or tag. Tell students to keep the information brief!

   Examples:

   —Peter Ashton    —Dr. Isaac Newton
      Vietnam              remembered for his ideas
      fighter pilot      about dropping apples

4. Ask the students to attach the labels to their clothing. They can use their own character or swap the labels around in the group. They should then stand up and move around, introducing pairs of students to each other *in terms of these identities*, for example: "Mr. Ashton, I wonder whether you have met Dr. Newton?" "Dr. Newton—Mr. Ashton." Let the activity slowly develop into a kind of cocktail party, with the students introducing each other, circulating, interrupting, and building on the information provided.

*Chris Mills*

# MAKING APPOINTMENTS VI-2

**Language Function(s):** Making appointments; socializing

**Materials:** Copies of an Appointment Book page (see page 68).

## Before Class

Make copies of the selected Appointment Book page.

## In Class

1. Pre-teach or "brainstorm" the language required for making appointments and build up a list of expressions on the board such as:

   —I have something I'd like to discuss with you.

   —When are you free?

   —I wonder if you could spare me a few minutes.

   —Could you make it on Monday? At 4 p.m.?

   —Yes/No, that would (not) be a convenient time.

2. Hand out the copies of the Appointment Book page. Ask the class to complete the dates or times on the page—(dates first version, times second version). Then ask the class to fill in a number of the spaces with imaginary appointments, for example: budget meeting, yoga, dentist, English lesson, and so on.

These appointments are fixed and cannot be changed. If pressed for time the class should simply cross out a number of spaces. Not all the spaces should be filled in, however; for example, with ten students, at least nine spaces should be left blank, with six students, at least five.

3. Ask the students to make appointments with each one of their classmates. This means that in a class of ten, each student has to make nine appointments. (Divide large classes into groups of about ten.) You can also take part yourself. Try to speak to all the students so you can check their English. It is fairly easy to make the first appointments, but as the number of free spaces dwindles, the language has to become more complicated. In the end, students may be forced to agree that it is impossible to arrange some meetings as things stand. This could lead to the students' rearranging the dates already made.

*Derek Risley*

## Editor's Note

In a class where I tried this recipe recently the students not only filled in who they were meeting, but in some cases added further details spontaneously. We then went through some of their appointments one by one for example: "On Monday morning I'm going shopping with Walter," or "On Tuesday afternoon I'm meeting Hubert at his place for coffee."

| APPOINTMENT BOOK (1) | | |
|---|---|---|
| Date | Morning | Afternoon |
| | | |
| | | |
| | | |
| | | |
| | | |

WEEKEND

| | | |
|---|---|---|
| | | |
| | | |
| | | |
| | | |
| | | |

| APPOINTMENT BOOK (2) | | | |
|---|---|---|---|
| 8−8.30 | | 12:30−1 | |
| 8:30−9 | | 1−1:30 | |
| | | | |
| | | | |
| | | | |
| | | | |
| | | | |
| | | | |
| | | | |
| | | | |

# TELEPHONE CONVERSATION

## VI-3

**Unit VI / STRUCTURES AND FUNCTIONS / Level: Intermediate / Time: 30 minutes**

**Language Function(s):** Socializing; exchanging information

**Materials:** None

### Before Class

Prepare a suitable telephone conversation which you can mime. It might be a good idea to use material from a textbook, although the activity works well with any telephone conversation as long as you can mime it clearly.

### In Class

1. Present your mime to the class. Concentrate your efforts on *one* of the two speakers, getting responses from the students and writing the speaker's words on the board. Leave blank spaces for the second speaker's contribution. Allow time for practicing the intonation patterns and expressive voice tones. Try to introduce all the material by means of mime, for example, make the gesture of writing for "Could you spell that, please?" or tap your wrist to elicit "What time?" You can also establish the situation of making a phone call by picking up an imaginary receiver and moving your hand in a dialing motion.

2. Go through the whole conversation from the beginning so that the class is thoroughly prepared both in what is written and in the missing half. Tell students to observe carefully, but do not let them write down any part of the conversation at this time. Now ask the students to practice in pairs. One of the partners reads the written part while the other tries to fill in the second speaker's lines, that is those that are missing. Pairs that work quickly can change parts so that they both get a turn while the others finish.

3. Ask the class to provide the missing language and write it on the board in the spaces you have left. Accept any responses that make sense in the context even if they differ from your original script. You might also let the students come to the front one by one and each write one of the responses. Once everything is correct, give the class the go-ahead to copy the material into their notebooks.

*William Atkinson*

# VI-4 MAKING REQUESTS

**Unit VI / STRUCTURES AND FUNCTIONS / Level: Intermediate / Time: 20 minutes**

**Language Function(s):** Making requests; adapting language to social role

**Materials:**
    a. A recording of some common sounds which require a response of some kind, such as a kettle whistling, a baby crying, a telephone ringing, a car honking its horn, a doorbell ringing and so on.
    b. Flash cards illustrating different social roles or emotions. Use drawings or magazine pictures as illustrations. For example:

| neutral social register: | formal social register: |
|---|---|
| family maid or baby sitter | employer |
| secretary | formidable mother-in-law |
| informal social register: | anger |
| brother or sister | love |
| friend | |

## Before Class

Prepare the materials needed as described.

## In Class

1. Present the recorded sounds and ask students of what they represent. Check effective recognition and teach any necessary vocabulary such as "the kettle's *whistling*." Then present the role cards and establish their significance by asking students to guess what sort of person or situation they represent. Don't worry too much if the students fall back on stereotypes at this stage. Make sure they appreciate the different language that would be used when talking to such a variety of people.

2. Play one sound effect and show one role card, for example, the phone ringing and the secretary. Ask for an appropriate (neutral) response such as "Would you answer the phone please?" Then change the role card to the friend, for example, and say, "The phone's ringing" to show that this can also be used as a request to answer the telephone in an informal situation. Build up a table of responses on the board.

3. Show the role card symbolizing anger and say "Answer the phone, will you?" using appropriate intonation to show anger. Vary the combination of sound effects and role cards to provide cues for further teacher-student practice, gradually developing into student-student practice. You might like to try adding to the initial responses so as to build up short dialogues such as:

    (Car honks its horn. Role card indicates friend or relative.)

    —Alistair's here. He's honking for you.

    —Can you tell him I'll be down in ten minutes. I'm taking a bath.

    —OK.

4. Round off the exercise with a discussion of cases in which *the situation* rather than someone's words requires us to say something. Examples might include a roof beginning to leak, change in the weather, knock at the door, malfunctioning machine and so on. What requests would be appropriate in these cases?

*Alan Cunningsworth*

**Unit VI / STRUCTURES AND FUNCTIONS / Level: Intermediate and above /
Time: 15–30 minutes**

**Language Function(s):** Interrupting; countering interruptions

**Materials:**     Copies of Worksheets 1 and 2

## Before Class

Prepare copies of Worksheets 1 and 2 which you can find following this recipe. Select a suitable text to read or prepare yourself to speak on a subject for five minutes.

## In Class

1. Hand out copies of Worksheet (see page 72) and work through it with the class. Explain the differences between the various interruptions. Which are formal and which informal? Which could you use and which not use when speaking to a superior? How does intonation affect the formality of an interruption?

2. Tell the class you are going to talk for about five minutes and that they should try to interrupt you *as much as possible*, using the phrases on the worksheet. The students can all interrupt together—the more expressions they call out the better. Counter the interruptions with replies such as those on Worksheet 2 (see page 72).

3. Distribute copies of Worksheet 2. Discuss the vocabulary and explain any new words and phrases. Divide the class into groups of four or five. Give the students a few minutes to prepare a talk or give them a passage to read aloud. Then ask the students in each group to read their passage or give their talks one by one while the others interrupt them as described in steps 1 and 2. They should also counter the interruptions as outlined above. Allow each student about two minutes and then go straight on to the next one, keeping the pace brisk.

## Author's Note

The aim of the exercise is to teach students to interrupt politely. It is intended to provide them with alternatives to the kind of interruptions one hears even from advanced students, and which may sound rude even if they are not intended to. The exercise can be used as a preliminary to a round-table meeting, role-playing activity or discussion.

*Jim Brims*

## 'Interrupting'—Student's Worksheet (1)

Your teacher is going to start reading or speaking on a particular subject. You should try to interrupt him or her as often as you can. Put a check ( √ ) next to each of the phrases as you hear it. You should try to use each of the phrases at least once.

**Phrases for interrupting:**

I wonder if I could just interrupt you there . . .

Could I interrupt to say . . .

Do you mind if I say something here?

Sorry to butt in, but . . .

Excuse me for interrupting you, but . . .

I'm sorry to interrupt your presentation, but . . .

If I could just say something here . . .

I don't want to hold us up, but . . .

**Asking for clarification:**

I wonder if I could ask for clarification on that point?

Could you be a little more specific?

I wonder if you should give us an example of that?

I'm afraid I didn't quite get that.

**Expressing opposition or disagreement:**

I'm afraid I don't agree with that . . .

Look, that really isn't quite right . . .

I don't see how it's possible to say that . . .

Yes, but on the other hand . . .

I really don't see how you can justify that.

**Contradiction:**

Yes, but if you say that the logical conclusion is . . .

You don't seriously think that, do you?

That can't possibly be right.

**Annoyance:**

Excuse me, but you really mustn't talk nonsense.

Don't give me that rubbish!

---

## 'Interrupting'—Student's Worksheet (2)

Now it is your turn to read or speak about a subject for two minutes. It does not need to be an interesting subject. You will have to read or speak while the others interrupt you. Here are some useful phrases to counter the interruptions.

If you will allow me to continue . . .

I wonder if I could explain that point later . . .

If I could explain that at the end . . .

Just a moment, please, I won't be long.

I wonder if I could continue with what I'm saying . . .

I'll be glad to clarify any points at the end.

# MODAL DRAWINGS

**Unit VI / STRUCTURES AND FUNCTIONS / Level: Intermediate / Time: 30 minutes**

**Language Function(s):** Expressing possibility, impossibility, necessity, and disbelief; making guesses and suppositions

**Materials:** None

## Before Class

Practice drawing the sequence of pictures on page 74.

## In Class

1. Tell the class you want to practice modal verbs such as may, might, must, could, can't, etc. There are several ways in which the students can work. You can divide the students into pairs or small groups which later pool their ideas, or you can work with the class as a whole and control the lesson.

2. Draw picture number 1 on the board and ask the class to use modals to comment on it. Accept statements such as "He's lying down" but encourage the students to concentrate on the modals, and to produce sentences like "He might have hurt himself" or "He could have fallen down." You can find further examples on the following page. Collect as many sentences as you can.

3. Continue in the same way adding further details, step by step, as shown in pictures 2 through 5. (This procedure should be clarified by the sequence of pictures.) It is important to elicit the material *from the students*. Do not simply recite a stream of your own ideas, although you should prompt and encourage the class if they lack inspiration.

4. Finish the activity with one or both of the following suggestions:

   a. Have the students tell the story, orally or in writing, either to a partner or the whole group. They should establish the causes of what happened.

   b. Have the groups produce new situations for which they produce their own drawings. Each group then elicits a story from the rest of the class.

*Ian Butcher*

He might be sleeping.
He may even be dead.
He could just be resting.

He might be unconscious.
He must have been hit with the plant pot.
He could be seeing stars.

The plant pot must have fallen from the window.
The wind could have blown the window open.
Someone might have thrown the plant pot at him.

He can't have been killed by the plant pot.
He might have been shot.

This man must have shot him.
He must have had a motive.
But he *can't* be dead! (With appropriate intonation.)

# THE FIRST AND SECOND CONDITIONALS

**Unit VI / STRUCTURES AND FUNCTIONS / Level: Intermediate / Time: 20 minutes**

**Language Function(s):** Expressing consequences under given conditions

**Materials:** None

**In Class**

1. Discuss what the members of the class habitually do and are likely to do again in the near future. You need to do this exercise with a class that has been working together for some time so that the students know each other well. Write five or six examples on the board, such as: Brigitte always chews gum, Jean stares out of the window, and Heinz always asks lots of questions. Ask for additional examples and add them on the board.

2. Ask the students how they will react if one of the people mentioned behaves as described, for example:

   —If Hilde speaks German in class tomorrow, I'll scream.

   —If Bob chews gum with his mouth open again, I'll move to another seat.

3. Change the names in the examples so that the habits are attributed to *other* students to whom they do not normally apply. This establishes a situation where the *second* conditional is required, for example:

   —If Ingrid spoke German in class tomorrow, I would scream.
   —If Billy chewed gum with his mouth open, I would move to another seat.

   Pay particular attention to the stressed pronunciation of "would." Be sure to point out that in normal speech it would be contracted to " 'd."

4. Allow the exercise to open up naturally—you need *not* respond to the same behavior in the same way if it is displayed by different people, for example:

   —If Heinz doesn't stop asking me for answers, I'll scream. But if Sonia kept asking me for the answers, I might ask her for a date.

   —If Renata tries to get another cigarette from me, I'll tell her to get lost. But if Teresa tried to get a cigarette from me, I'd give her the whole pack.

   Once again, be sure not to neglect to practice the stress and intonation, which is particularly important in such contrastive examples.

   *Mike Levy*

**Language Function(s):** Completing sentences; asking questions

**Materials:**   None

## Before Class

Go through material already studied and make a selection of statements and questions students should be able to complete.

Write them out clearly and prepare them thoroughly.

Blank out the last part of each sentence, leaving, for example:

−How can I . . . .

−He should be . . . .

−I can't . . . .

−We were able to . . . .

−You have to understand . . . .

−She will tell you when to . . . .

## In Class

1. Read the examples one by one, or hand out a list and ask the students to complete them. Obviously, since the statements are all open-ended, there are numerous possible ways of completing them. Circulate, helping as necessary. When the students are ready, ask them to read their sentences aloud. Allow several students to complete an item before going on to the next one. For more advanced groups, encourage longer sentences. The exercise should be done *quickly* or it won't be much fun.

2. Another review exercise is to list the answers to a selection of questions in structures the students have studied. They must then supply a question that would fit a given answer. In many cases there are several suitable possibilities as some answers, like those given below, clearly permit a wide range of questions.

| Answer | Possible Questions |
|---|---|
| −No, I can't | −Can you swim/drive a car/say the alphabet backwards/stand on your head? |
| −Mary | −Who's that? What are you going to call the baby if it's a girl? What's your sister's name? |
| −18 | −How old are you? How much is 9 + 9? How many cousins do you have? |
| −I don't believe it! | −Did you know I'm saving up to buy a helicopter? Did I tell you I'm going to the moon on vacation? |
| −Yes, you should | −Should I apply for that job? Should I come round tomorrow? |

Again, this exercise should be done *rapidly*. Have all your cues written out beforehand so that you don't get confused and break the rhythm.

*Carlos Maeztu*

## Editor's Note

This technique is described in greater detail in the following recipe, ''Questions and Answers.''

# VI-9

# QUESTIONS AND ANSWERS

## Unit VI / STRUCTURES AND FUNCTIONS / Level: Intermediate / Time: 45 minutes

**Language Function(s):** Asking questions

**Materials:** None

### Before Class

Prepare a list of answers, the questions to which should allow the students to use certain forms of structures which they have already encountered. For example, "Right, then turn left at the traffic lights," to which a suitable question might be something like "How do I get to Fifth Avenue?"

Unless you have decided to work on only one particular structure, try to prepare answers which test the whole range of question and verb forms so far covered by the class, for example:

| Answer | Possible Questions? |
|---|---|
| —I was held up by the traffic | —Why were you late?<br>—Why didn't you arrive on time?<br>—Why didn't you call? |
| —She burst into tears | —What happened when she realized she'd lost her passport?<br>—How did she react when she heard she'd won the scholarship? |
| —Ever since I was a child | —Have you always been allergic to pollen?<br>—How long have you been learning the guitar? |

### In Class

1. Distribute the list of answers you have prepared as a handout or write it on the board. Students can work singly, in pairs or in small groups. Their task is to prepare suitable questions for these answers. (See the examples in the table above.) If some students finish before others, tell them to think of further, alternative questions. Circulate, helping as necessary. Write the best answers on the board.

2. Variations

   a. With more advanced classes this technique can also be employed to practice idiomatic phrases in the same way. Ask the students to provide suit-able prompts for such expressions as: "Never mind." "Come off it," "You gotta be kidding!" or "No way!" Other good examples would be: "Certainly not!" "They moo," "Serves you right!" "65 miles," "With two t's," and so on.

   b. The students can also be asked to make a list of answers which are then distributed to other students to be "solved" as described in step 1.

   c. This variation is particularly well suited to "getting to know you" sessions at the beginning of a term or course. Ask the students to write down ten facts about themselves as short answers, for example: "21," "Blue," "Zagreb," "1976," "Twice," "Torquay and London," "Zlata," "Fishing and ballet,'' ''Marlon Brando,'' ''Steak and Cheese.''

Divide the class into pairs. The partners must then make suggestions and try to establish the right questions to these answers.The answer ''1976'' might produce a conversation along the following lines:

A: Did you get married in 1976?

B: No, I didn't.

A: Perhaps you had a child?

B: No—not married, no children.

A: Was it at all connected with your family?

B: No. It was more to do with work.

A: You started work for the first time?

B: You're getting warmer . . .

A: Ah, I know! You graduated from college?

B: You got it!

Finally, armed with this information, each student tells the class something about the person he or she has been working with.

*Rick Haill*

# UNIT 7

# VOCABULARY (LEXIS)

**Unit VII / VOCABULARY (LEXIS) / Level: All / Time: 25 minutes**

**Language Function(s):** Making associations

**Materials:** None

**Before Class**

Select about 30 words which have already occurred in class and which you feel need review.

**In Class**

1. Write five of the words that need review on the board like this:

> seagull                                    stone
>
>
>                    confusion
>
>
> lamp                                      toenail

Ask the class to make word associations diagonally, starting in the corners and working toward the cen-

ter, so that each of the corner words eventually becomes linked up with the center word like this:

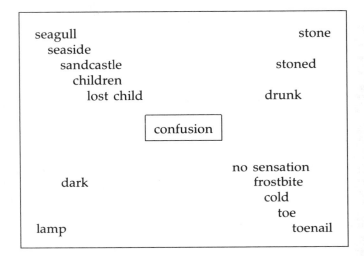

> seagull                                    stone
>   seaside
>     sandcastle                          stoned
>       children
>         lost child                       drunk
>
>                  confusion
>
>
>                                    no sensation
>        dark                          frostbite
>                                       cold
>                                        toe
> lamp                                  toenail

2. Give the students the list of words you have selected as needing review. Ask them to make *arbitrary* groups of five words from this selection and to write them down as above, that is with one in the middle and one in each corner. They should *not* begin by choosing five connected words. Then ask them to write their individual associations in the manner described.

3. After 10 to 15 minutes ask the class to compare their ideas and associations in pairs or small groups.

*Mike Lavery*

# VOCABULARY REVIEW

## Unit VII / VOCABULARY (LEXIS) / Level: Intermediate / Time: 30 minutes

**Language Function(s):** Making associations

**Materials:** Small cards

### Before Class

Prepare two *different* sets of 20 to 30 words written on cards (one word per card). It is a good idea to use different colored cards so that you can distinguish the sets easily. The words chosen should be mostly nouns that have occurred in previous lessons and now require review.

### In Class

1. Divide the class into two groups and give each group one of the sets of cards. Let the groups read aloud their words and then settle the meanings *among themselves* as far as possible. The other group should *not* know what the words are.

2. Tell each group to choose six of their words (one word for each student*) that they feel have related meanings. At first, the themes of the associations are often obvious, but when the activity is repeated the students usually try to find more imaginative connections.

3. Ask each student to write his or her word in a sentence. Thus both groups will have six sentences. Again it should *not* be obvious which word each sentence is formed around—see step 4. Tell the groups to exchange their sentences orally in pairs, with each student from group one working with a partner from group two.

4. Ask the students to re-form in their original groups. Each student is to report back with the sentence he or she has heard from the other group. It is a good idea for a group secretary to write the sentences down. Tell the students to look carefully at the six sentences and to try to find which words and associations the other group had chosen, and what their themes of association were.

### Author's Note

*The exercise as described here is intended for a group of twelve.

*Christine Frank*

**Unit VII / VOCABULARY (LEXIS) / Level: Intermediate and above /
Time: 50–60 minutes**

**Language Function(s):** Identifying and contrasting vocabulary

**Materials:** Slips of paper

## Before Class

a. Make a list of words that are commonly confused by students at the level you are teaching. Make sure you are able to give a clear explanation of the difference between the words; some of them are far more tricky than they appear. A sample of suggested confused words might be:

| | |
|---|---|
| rob/steal | presently/actually |
| passed/past | prevent/avoid |
| loose/lose | economic/economical |
| say/tell | principal/principle |
| adopt/adapt | human/humane |
| price/prize | error/fault |
| moral/morale | affect/effect |
| rise/raise | industrious/industrial |
| sensible/sensitive | opportunity/occasion |

b. Take some of the slips of paper and write three words from the list on each of them. You need one slip for each student. It may be necessary to duplicate some items, depending on the number of students in your class. Plan the selection of words so that both members of the pair of words you choose are included. Make sure you arrange the sets of words to facilitate interaction between as wide a range of students as possible. (See step 1.)

## In Class

1. Distribute one "mini list" of three words to each student. Explain that they must circulate and try to find words from the other students' pieces of paper, that are commonly confused with the ones they have on their own pieces of paper. Gino, for example, might have: AFFECT/INDUSTRIAL/OCCASION. His job is to find the three classmates who have: EFFECT, INDUSTRIOUS, and OPPORTUNITY. (This is why the words each student is looking for should be distributed among three different students on three different pieces of paper.) You should also circulate around the room, advising, listening and answering questions.

2. To introduce a competitive element, you may wish to stop when the first student has completed the task. Otherwise, continue until everyone has finished. Give those who are ready another example or two to keep them busy, but make sure you leave adequate time for illustration and explanation of all the words.

3. Ask the students to write a couple of sentences to bring out the different meanings of the words they have successfully matched. Go around the group and check what they have written. Finally, ask the students to read their words and sentences aloud and invite comment from the others. You may find that this activity prompts students to talk about other lexical points they find confusing.

*Rick Haill*

# THE CUT-OUT BEDROOM VII-4

**Language Function(s):** Expressing spatial relations; describing

**Materials:** Sets of materials, enough for one-third the number of people in the class, each set consisting of a large piece (ca. 9″ × 12″) of colored construction paper with a large rectangle drawn on it; several smaller pieces of contrasting-color paper; cutouts of a rug and a bed (seen from above, labeled) also in contrasting colors; felt pens; scissors.

## Before Class

Get the materials together in sets, making sure you have enough for groups of three students.

## In Class

1. Divide the class into groups of three or four, and give each group one of the sets of materials. Tell the students to do what they wish with the materials. (You may wish simply to distribute the materials, say nothing about them, and leave the room briefly, letting the class decide what they are going to do with the materials.) After discussion, students generally come up with the idea of planning a bedroom, although some groups may prefer to plan a different room or even a whole house.

2. If the students do not start planning a room (or house), suggest that they do so. While the students are discussing their plans (and making cutouts for other furniture) they will be thinking spatially and using spatial prepositions (for example, near, beside, in front of, behind). They will also be making group decisions about what is needed and where it is to be put. During this time, circulate around the room and elicit appropriate language such as "near wall," "far wall," and "top right-hand corner." Point out or elicit the relative nature of these expressions, that they differ depending on where the speaker and listener are located—for example the "near wall" to one person is the "far wall" to a person sitting opposite him or her.

3. When the groups have completed their plans, encourage them to look at other groups' efforts and discuss them with their creators.

## Author's Note

This activity serves as a valuable lead-in to the well-known exercise in which students sit back to back and take turns at describing their bedrooms while their partner draws the plan. I have found that the students get far more out of this exercise and are far more successful at it after doing "The Cut-Out Bedroom."

*Diane Fitton*

# VII-5 ## PRACTICING PHRASAL VERBS

**Unit VII / VOCABULARY (LEXIS) / Level: Intermediate and above /
Time: 60 – 90 minutes**

**Language Function(s):** Practicing phrasal verbs

**Materials:**  None

## In Class

1. Ask each student to bring between one and four
sentences which contain phrasal (two-part, two-
word) verbs to the next class. They should be clear
about the meaning and should be prepared to explain it. Typical examples would be: "Please *pick* me
*up* at 8.00 tomorrow," "I'll *take* you *on* at chess
anytime," "The meeting *broke up* earlier than ex-
pected."

2. At the next class, divide the students into groups of
about three or four. Ask the students to teach each
other their verbs. Quickly go around checking that
the verbs are used correctly, explaining as necessary and answering any questions.

3. When the groups are clear about the meanings, ask
them to make up stories including as many of their
phrasal verbs as possible. Tell them that each group

should be ready to mime its story to the rest of the
class. Circulate, again helping as necessary and dis-
creetly supervising the rehearsal of the miming once
the stories have been written.

4. Ask one group to act out its story in mime. The
others have to try to establish which phrasal verbs
are being depicted. Then have the group repeat its
mime. This time, the audience can "freeze" the
actors, ask them questions (which they can answer
verbally), and if possible, write the verbs on the
board as they come up.

5. If time and interest permit, let each group perform
while the others try to spot the phrasal verbs in the
same way. Make a note of all the verbs to practice
later. (Start by checking that they know them at the
next lesson.)

*Katya Benjamin*

## Publisher's Note

Lists of phrasal verbs are found in many sources including *Nelson Practice Book of
Phrasal Verbs* by Walker (Nelson), *Take it Easy: American Idioms* by McPartland
(Prentice-Hall), *Mastering American English* by Hayden, et al, (Prentice-Hall),
*Idiom Workbook* by Berman and Kirstein (Institute of Modern Language), *Diction-
ary of Two-Word Verbs for Students of English* by Eugene Hall (Minerva Books).

**SIGNS**

**Unit VII / VOCABULARY (LEXIS) / Level: Low intermediate to intermediate / Time: 30 minutes**

**Language Function(s):** Interpreting signs

**Materials:**   None

## In Class

1. "Brainstorm" signs, for example: Keep left; Keep off the grass; Wet paint; No trespassing; No Vacancies; and so on. Write the material on the board. Ask the class what they think the signs mean and where they might be found. Explain as necessary. For example, "'No Vacancies' would probably be seen in front of a motel or guest house and means that it is full."

2. Divide the class into pairs or threes and tell them to prepare a mime or short skit to illustrate one of the signs. For instance, to illustrate "No Vacancies," one student might play the part of a tourist looking for a room with another as a hotel manager or clerk.

3. Have each group perform its skit. The actors should not specify what sign is being represented, as it is the task of the rest of the class to guess what it is.

4. As a follow-up, you may wish to have the students go out and note two or three new signs for discussion at the next class. If you are teaching in a country where there are no English signs, tell the students to collect the signs in whatever languages they can. Their task at the next class will then be to translate them into English.

5. Another productive idea is to ask the students to think up new signs for anything they might like to stop, promote, or draw people's attention to. They should explain why they feel these signs are necessary, so that the activity can be rounded off with a lively discussion. The signs could be written on pieces of paper and put on the classroom walls.

*Richard Baudains*

# VOCABULARY EXPANSION

**Unit VII / VOCABULARY (LEXIS) / Level: Intermediate / Time: 45 minutes**

**Language Function(s):** Categorizing vocabulary

**Materials:** Large sheets of paper; felt-tip pens

## In Class

1. Ask for two student volunteers, one who likes drawing and one with clear handwriting. Get the artist to start drawing a courtroom and the people in it. As he or she draws, the "secretary" should write in the names of the parts of the room such as "bench" and "witness stand" and the descriptions of the people, for instance, "judge" and "defense attorney." When the secretary does not know a word, he or she should ask the class, or as a last resort, the teacher.

2. Distribute the sheets of paper and felt-tip pens. Ask the students to copy the blackboard drawing, writing in the nouns needed to designate the places and people in the appropriate places. This is to consolidate the vocabulary that has been introduced in step 1.

3. Tell the students you are going out for five minutes. When you come back you want them to have organized themselves into a courtroom, with different students taking different roles and standing or sitting in the appropriate parts of the room. When you come back into the room, go up to the students and ask them questions such as: "Where are you?" "Who are you?" "Who do you like in this room?" or "Who do you sympathize with?" This activates the vocabulary generated and sets it in an affective frame by making the students take on the parts of the defendant, witnesses, jury, and so on. It is important to note, however, that this activity is not intended as a straightforward role-playing exercise.

4. Tell the students to return to their seats and to organize the courtroom vocabulary they know into categories. The only rule is that they must *put each word into at least two categories.* (For example, "witness stand" could go into a category of "furniture" and one of "connected with the defendant.") It is important *not* to give examples of what you mean by categories—let the students work it out for themselves. When they have organized the words into their own categories, get the students to read out their lists. This gives you a final check on pronunciation and stress. Allow students to ask for an explanation of each other's classification but be sure they respect each other's personal associations.

## Author's Note

This exercise owes a lot to Caleb Gattegno's ideas. The categorization technique comes straight from *The Silent Way.*

## Editor's Note

This is a shorter version of an article in Frank and Rinvolucri *Grammar in Action* (Pergamon.)

*Mario Rinvolucri*

# ERBS IN MOTION

**Unit VII / VOCABULARY (LEXIS) / Level: Intermediate and above / Time: Sessions of 15 minutes**

**Language Function(s):** Describing movement

**Materials:** Selection of verbs of motion with illustrations

## Before Class

Prepare a list of verbs of motion geared to the level of your class together with suitable situational prompts (cues) or illustrations to accompany them. Plan the material to be spread over several sessions depending on the group. (Remember that it has been estimated that the average student can absorb a maximum of only seven new words of expressions in any one lesson.)

## In Class

1. Let the class choose a name, say Pat, to provide a focal character for the basic sentence, which should be written on the board like this:

    Pat . . . . . . . . . along the road.
    
    ↑
    (verb)

    Begin by giving a simple example such as "Pat was in a car." Here a suitable verb is "drove," so that the model becomes:

    Pat *drove* along the road.

    Or, if Pat were drunk, the model would be:

    Pat *staggered*, or *lurched*, or *tottered* along the road.

## Suggested List of Prompts and Verbs

Pat was . . . .

1. in a car = drove
2. in a very fast car = sped/raced
3. in an old car = squeaked/rattled
4. in an old car on a bad road = bumped/jolted
5. on a bicycle = cycled/pedaled
6. an old man on an old bike = wobbled
7. on a fast motorcycle = sped/zoomed/hurtled
8. on a pony = trotted
9. riding a horse quite quickly = cantered
10. on a race horse = galloped

There is a list of fifty suggested prompts (cues) and verbs at the end of this recipe.

2. Act out or illustrate the verbs as you give the prompts, and explain them as necessary. Except with very advanced classes it is advisable to give the students a list of the verbs you have chosen. This may be done in advance, so that they can mull over them. It should ensure that more verbs will be produced by the students and that they can contribute more to the discussion of similarities and differences among the verbs. To round off each session, reverse the procedure: give students the verbs and ask them to recall the prompts or situations like this:

    Pat *drove* along the road.        She was in a car.

    Pat *staggered* along the road.        She was drunk.

3. As a follow-up, either choose students who enjoy acting and get them to act out some of the verbs from your list, or mime the action yourself. In either case, have the students guess the verbs. Groups can also be asked to work out a short mime story which they then present to the class. The other students are then asked to describe the action, using the new vocabulary wherever possible.

11. a soldier = marched/paraded
12. a policeman = patrolled/proceeded
13. in no hurry = ambled/strolled/sauntered
14. lame = hobbled/limped
15. very tired = plodded/trudged
16. very old = shuffled
17. a baby = toddled/crawled
18. very proud and self-important = swaggered/strutted
19. a happy little boy = hopped/skipped

20. trying to keep fit = jogged
21. in training for the hundred meters = sprinted/sped
22. leading a cavalry attack = charged
23. a burglar = stole/prowled/crept
24. a ballet dancer = leaped/pirouetted
25. in a good mood = breezed/cavorted/frolicked
26. in a bad mood = stomped/stamped
27. an acrobat = cartwheeled/somersaulted
28. in a Rolls Royce = glided
29. driving a tank or a bulldozer = rumbled
30. in a steam engine = chugged

31. The road was icy = She slipped/slid
32. The road was deep in snow = She trudged/skied/slogged
33. The road was two feet deep in water = She waded
34. It was pitch dark and/or a thick fog = She groped/felt her way
35. She didn't want to disturb anyone = She tiptoed

And some less serious ones . . . . .

Pat was . . . .

36. a slob = drooled
37. a fox = slunk/sneaked
38. a snake = slithered
39. a butterfly = fluttered
40. wearing very high heels = teetered/wobbled
41. a member of the Reichswehr = goosestepped
42. Pele (or any famous soccer player) = dribbled
43. Scott Hamilton or Dorothy Hamill (or any famous figure skater) = skated/glided/twirled
44. John Travolta = shimmied/rocked/gyrated
45. lost or a poet = wandered/meandered
46. a student trying to hitch a ride = hitchhiked/hitched/thumbed
47. overweight or a duck = waddled
48. into levitation = floated
49. acting suspiciously = sidled
50. on an airplane = jetted/streaked

*Rick Haill*

**Unit VII / VOCABULARY (LEXIS) / Level: Intermediate and above / Time: 2 sessions, one of 60 minutes and one of 45 minutes**

**Language Function(s):** Describing movement

**Materials:** For the second session you need cards with verbs written on them as described below

## Before Class

Make sure you can mime or explain any words that might come up. Prepare the cards for the second session—see step 5.

## In Class

1. Draw a diagram showing two localities, for example, a house and a supermarket, or simply A and B, on the board. Tell the class you want to look at some of the different ways we can go from one place to another, for example "run" or "stagger." You can find some more examples in List A at the end of this recipe. Pick out a suitable selection for your group.

2. Ask the students to come up in twos and threes and write as many verbs of motion as they can think of on the board. If they do not know the exact word they want they should either draw the action or write a clue, for instance, "on one leg" instead of "hop." Prompt as necessary with examples such as "The sidewalk was icy," or "What if you're old and tired?" or "Say you're on a bicycle," and so on.

3. Discuss the words and their application. Decide on clues as to the meanings and write or draw them on the board beside the relevant words, for example: "rush" = "he was in a hurry" or ⌐┘ ⅀ = "crawl." Then erase either the clues, leaving only the verbs, or the verbs leaving only the clues. Go through them with the class.

4. As an initial follow-up, divide the class into two teams, each of which has to make a list of ten to twelve verbs from those covered in the lesson. A member of team A must then mime a word given him or her by team B *to his or her own team*, who have to guess it. Team B may choose to give either the verb itself or the clue as the answer. Then the other team has a turn and so on.

5. Several lessons later, follow up by dividing the class into two teams or groups. Give each group a card with a selection of items from the suggestions in List B. (You can find even more examples in the recipe "Verbs in Motion" on page 89.) The cards should be different, and one or two new verbs may be included. Separate the groups, sending one group out of the room if possible. Quickly check that the students know all the verbs on their cards and that they can mime them. Then have each group take turns at miming its verbs for the other students to guess. The comic aspect of this activity helps impress the words on the students' memories.

## List A—Suggested Verbs For Part 1 (Step 1 to 4)

| | | | | |
|---|---|---|---|---|
| amble | hop | plod | slide | trudge |
| bump | hurtle | race | slip | wade |
| crawl | jog | ride | sprint | wander |
| creep | jolt | sail | stagger | weave |
| gallop | limp | shuffle | strol | zigzag |
| hobble | pedal | skip | tiptoe | zoom |

(Naturally you do not have to teach *all* these verbs, particularly if your class knows hardly any of them.)

## List B—Suggestions For Part 2 (Step 5)

He or She was . . .

—training for the 100 meters = sprinted

—depressed and tired = trudged

—lame = limped

—in a hurry = ran

—not in a hurry = strolled

—on a bike for the first time = wobbled

—wounded in the stomach and unable to get to his or her feet = dragged himself or herself

—on a road two feet deep in water = waded

—full of himself or herself = sauntered

—on a racehorse = galloped

—on a motorbike = zoomed

—a burglar moving stealthily = crept

## Author's Note

This approach to teaching verbs of motion developed from using the ideas described in my husband's recipe "Verbs of Motion" (see page 89.)

*Alison Haill*

# UNIT 8

# FUN AND GAMES

# VIII-1 PICTURE DIALOGUE GAME

**Unit VIII / FUN AND GAMES / Level: Low intermediate / Time: 20 minutes**

**Language Function(s):** Writing dialogues

**Materials:** Large pictures each showing two people talking

### In Class

1. Bring in six to ten pictures, each one showing two people talking, and put them up at the front of the class. Make sure that all the students can see them clearly.

2. Arrange the students in pairs and ask each pair to choose one of the pictures to use as the basis of a short dialogue. The rest of the group should not know which pictures have been chosen. Give the students three or four minutes to write down what they think the two people in the picture are saying. Circulate, checking that the language is correct and helping as necessary.

3. Ask the pairs to read or, better still, act out their dialogues, each partner taking one role while the rest of the class tries to guess which picture has been chosen. Whenever possible, the students should justify their guesses.

*Christine Frank*

# PICTURE QUESTION GAME

**Unit VIII / FUN AND GAMES / Level: Low intermediate to intermediate / Time: 30—45 minutes**

**Language Function(s):** Asking and answering questions

**Materials:** Pictures as described below

## Before Class

Cut out three fairly detailed pictures from a magazine. Street scenes or household interiors which contain a lot of detail are most suitable.

## In Class

1. Hold up one of the pictures to the class for about 45—60 seconds. Then put the picture down where no one can see it and ask memory questions such as: "What color is the . . . . . ?" "How many . . . are there?" "What's on the right of the . . . . . . ?" and so on. Tailor your questions to the needs and level of your class. You may wish to show the picture two or even three times, following each showing with further questions as described above.

2. Divide the class into two teams, A and B. Give each team one picture. Tell them to prepare twelve memory questions for the other team to answer. Go around and check that the questions are in correct English.

3. Team A is shown team B's picture for up to a minute. Team B now ask its questions, which team A has to answer. Award points for correct answers. Write the points on the board or get one of the students to do so. The questioning can take place in several ways:

   a. Team B members can take turns asking the questions with team A members either answering in turn or working together as a panel.

   b. You may also pair students from the teams so that each student works with a partner from the opposing team. This maximizes student participation, since *each* student asks, or has to answer, *all twelve* questions. If the class works this way, it is of course essential for each team member to have all the questions in written form.

   c. Each member of team B takes two or three questions and asks them of team A, one by one.

   After the questioning, however it is done, Team A should be allowed to see the picture again to check both the points its members had not remembered and those that they had.

4. Now show Team A's picture to Team B, and repeat Step 3 with Team A as inquisitors and Team B as respondents.

*Saxon Menné*

# VIII-3 PICTURE GAME

**Language Function(s):** Describing; asking questions; evaluating content

**Materials:** One or two interesting pictures, preferably mounted on cardboard

## In Class

1. Explain the activity clearly to the class. Tell them you are going to give a picture to one pair of students so that only they can see it. Both of them will then offer what is claimed to be a description of the picture, but only *one* description will be accurate. The other account will be invented. After each of the two students has offered his or her description, the rest of the class should ask questions to try and determine which account is real and which is imagined.

2. Select the pair of students and give them a picture. If it isn't mounted you may need a piece of cardboard to hold behind it to ensure that it remains secret—the class should not be able to see through it if it is held up to the light.

3. Ask the two students to decide quietly who will invent and who will tell the truth. Then have them prepare their description. (This might be assigned as homework so they will have enough time to prepare their accounts in more detail.)

4. The two chosen students should present their descriptions to the class. Should the pace lag when the questions are being asked, or should the class be certain that they have found out the truth, stop and ask why they think what they do. Discourage answers like, "Well, I just think so." The students should try to give reasons for their opinions.

5. Show the class the picture, and discuss its content. If interest is high, you may wish to select another pair and repeat the exercise with a different picture.

*Randal Holme*

# GUESS THE OBJECT — VIII-4

Unit VIII / FUN AND GAMES / Level: Intermediate / Time: 20 minutes

**Language Function(s):** Describing

**Materials:** Slips of paper with object names

## Before Class

Prepare some slips of paper with the names of objects written on them, for example: electric blanket, lipstick, television set, and pair of binoculars. Fold the slips in two so that the writing cannot be seen. The vocabulary should be restricted to objects that the students know and can identify in English.

## In Class

1. Teach or review spatial relationships between objects and lines and various related vocabulary. Expressions that the students will need to use might include:

   above, below, at right angles, parallel, on the left/

   right, higher, lower, further up/down/left/right,

   round, square, rectangular, triangular, etc.

2. Ask a student who can draw to go to the board. Ask another student, or perhaps a pair of students, to take one of the slips of paper at random. This student's (or pair's) task is to describe the object written on the slip, *without saying anything about its func-tion.* In other words, a ruler should be described as "having a series of regular marks along its side" and *not* as "an object for measuring things." A television set is described as "one square (the screen) within a rectangle (the cabinet) with some small circles (the controls) in one of the corners."

3. The "artists" must try to draw what is described while the rest of the class use this drawing together with the oral description to guess what the object is. The student(s) dictating the description should correct the artist by giving further instructions, for example, "No, the second rectangle is smaller," or "Put it a little further over to the left" and so on.

4. The student who first guesses the object correctly picks another slip at random and the activity continues. You may wish to have this student choose a partner to work with. The activity is far more demanding than it sounds if the rule about not saying anything about the objects' functions is strictly adhered to.

*Miranda Britt*

**Unit VIII / FUN AND GAMES / Level: All / Time: 20 minutes**

**Language Function(s):** Making guesses and suppositions; expressing (im)possibility and necessity

**Materials:**    Large bag or box

## In Class

1. Tell the students to each choose an object which they have with them, but not to let anyone else see it. Go around the room collecting the objects in a suitable container, not forgetting to put in something of your own. If you have a very small class, say six students or fewer, you may wish to ask for two objects from each participant.

2. Either empty the contents of the container onto the table or take the objects out one by one. Be careful—some people may have put in something fragile such as a watch. Make it clear that the students should *not* say which objects are theirs at this stage.

3. Work through the objects individually, asking the class to name or describe each one, and build up a list on the board. Elicit the vocabulary from the class as far as possible. Encourage the students to describe the objects as well as name them.

4. Tell the class that their next task is to establish which objects belong to which people. Take them one by one.

   *With beginning or low-intermediate groups,* use formulas such as: "This is--------'s" or "I think this is---------'s." The students should give reasons wherever possible. This can be done quite simply:

   Peter: I think the cigarette lighter is Angela's.

Angela: But I don't smoke.

Rosa: I think it's Manfred's. He smokes.

Manfred: Look—my matches. I think it's Barbara's because only she and I smoke in this group.

In this short example Barbara can now admit that it is hers. Make sure there is always a lot of discussion and speculation before the students claim their objects.

*With higher level groups,* use combinations of the following structures:

"It may/might/could/must/can't/couldn't be------'s (because) . . . . . ."

For example:

Christine: It looks like a man's watch, but as some women wear larger watches these days, it *could* belong to a woman.

Frank: Yes, but all of us are wearing watches except Richard, so it *must* be his.

The activity finishes when all the objects have been claimed.

*Saxon Menné and Christine Frank*

# IF I WERE YOU . . . .

**Unit VIII / FUN AND GAMES / Level: Intermediate / Time: 20 minutes**

**Language Function(s):** Speculating; expressing consequences

**Materials:**    None

## In Class

1. In this game one member of the group is sent out of the classroom while the others decide on a profession which that person is to assume. When the person comes back, the others must make subtle remarks using the structure "If I were you . . . ." For example, if it has been decided that the person is a boxer, the students might say:

   "If I were you I'd jump rope every day."
   "If I were you I'd give up smoking."

   A few of these examples should be prepared while the person is still outside. Don't let the class choose a profession for which nobody can think of anything to say! It is also important to avoid obvious examples such as: "If I were you I'd serve meals in a restaurant all day."

2. Call back the person who was sent out. This student's task now is to find out what his or her assumed profession is. The person can ask the others questions using "If you were me would you . . . . ?"

to try to establish the designated profession. Some examples might be: "If you were me, would you work outdoors or indoors?" "Would you make a lot of money?" "Would you have to be able to type?" (It is also a good idea to tell the one who is "it" to prepare similar questions while he or she is out. This provides something for the person to do while waiting and should help to keep things moving while the game is going on.)

3. If the group gets stuck, try helping by slipping them pieces of paper with ideas on them, say "gloves," "lose weight," or "look ugly" for the boxer. You can also send the person out again and re-prime the group if things have reached a standstill. Another possibility if the class loses ideas, is to make the one who is "it" turn his or her back while you mime relevant cues such as a waiter carrying a tray, writing down an order, or taking a fly out of somebody's soup!

*Ian Butcher*

**Unit VIII / FUN AND GAMES / Level: Low intermediate to advanced / Time: 20 minutes**

**Language Function(s):** Appreciating grammar

**Materials:** None

### In Class

1. Ask the class to write any grammar points they are not sure of on pieces of paper, which you should then collect. Typical examples might be "the conditional" or "used to." Go through the points, either quickly during the class, or as preparation for a later lesson if you feel unsure of your knowledge of English grammar. Then select *one* point which you can explain clearly and which you feel can be used productively in the way described below.

2. Ask one student to leave the room with the task of preparing as many questions as possible about anything. There should be no restrictions concerning the subject matter. Meanwhile, go over the grammar point you have selected with the rest of the group. Whenever possible let those students who understand the point explain it to the others.

3. Bring the student back in, and have him or her ask the questions. The others have to reply *using the tense or grammar point that is being practiced* in as natural a sentence as they can. For instance, if you were doing the conditional and the question was "What are you doing tomorrow?" the answer might be: I'll be sitting here working as usual but if I'd taken that other job I was offered I'd probably have gone on vacation." The next question might be: "What do you think about nuclear power?" to which suitable replies would be: "I'd have been much happier if it had been prohibited years ago" or "If it hadn't been for the accident at Three Mile Island, I think I'd probably still be in favor of it." The replies may be true or imaginary. The questioner has to guess which structure has been chosen. The object of the game is to think of a variety of contexts for the use of the point being practiced.

*Marjorie Baudains*

# GRAMMATICAL SNAKES AND LADDERS

**Unit VIII / FUN AND GAMES / Level: All / Time: 35 minutes**

---

**Language Function(s):** Asking questions

**Materials:** A copy of the playing board (p. 102), a die, and a set of rules (p. 103) for each group of four students; one counter for each student

## Before Class

Make copies of the materials required. Optionally, design your own version of the game—see the Author's Note below.

## In Class

1. Divide the class into fours, and give each group a die, a copy of the board, and a set of rules. Give each student a plastic counter. If no counters are available, the students can use different coins or simply write their initials on small squares of paper or cardboard.

2. Tell the students to read the rules and start playing. Keep well in the background. Intervene only when a group cannot decide if a sentence is correct or when they have made an incorrect decision. Try not to interrupt, but keep an ear open for points you might want to work on in later lessons.

3. When the game is over, go through the sentences, or at least ask if there are any sentences which the students still are not sure of. If one group finishes a long time before the others, they may be asked to plan their own snakes and ladders board while the others finish.

## Author's Note

There is no reason why other boards, based on the same rules, but focusing on other language fields, should not be constructed. For example, one could easily design a board to deal with the specific language problems of Turks or Japanese, directing attention to the definite and indefinite articles.

*Mario Rinvolucri*

## Editor's Note

This recipe is a somewhat shorter version of the author's "Snakes and Ladders" in his book *Grammar Games* (Pilgrims Publications, Canterbury, U.K.)

| | | | | | |
|---|---|---|---|---|---|
| | | FINISH 70 | Do your friend want to stay? 69 | They came? 68 | Why didn't you was able to come? 67 |
| Which of them liked you best? 61 | 62 | How many does she wants? 63 | 64 | How about dropping around to see us? 65 | Who ate what? 66 |
| 60 | Which car liked you best? 59 | 58 | Who told him that? 57 | 56 | Why said he that? 55 |
| 49 | 50 | Must you really go? 51 | 52 | Did he wanted to see me? 53 | 54 |
| Why not tell them? 48 | 47 | Do you must tell her? 46 | 45 | What did you want? 44 | 43 |
| What does he think? 37 | 38 | What happened? 39 | 40 | They not like me? 41 | 42 |
| 36 | 35 | What want you? 34 | 33 | Can you come with me tonight? 32 | 31 |
| 25 | What you think? 26 | 27 | Who did you speak to? 28 | 29 | Who came? 30 |
| Why did she come? 24 | 23 | Was they with us? 22 | 21 | Spoke they at the meeting? 20 | 19 |
| Did he was here yesterday? 13 | 14 | 15 | Who spoke at the meeting? 16 | 17 | Did she spoke at the meeting? 18 |
| 12 | Was he here yesterday? 11 | 10 | He was here yesterday? 9 | 8 | 7 |
| START 1 | Do you can come with me tonight? 2 | 3 | Do you like coffee? 4 | 5 | Do your parent like coffee? 6 |

## The Rules

1. All put your counters on start.

2. Decide who is going to begin and in which order you are are going to play.

3. If you are the first player, roll your die and move forward the number of squares indicated.

4. If you land on a sentence, say if it is correct or not. If you think there is a mistake in the sentence, correct it immediately.

5. Your group must then decide if you are right or not. (Ask your teacher only if you are completely unable to arrive at a decision.) If your group agrees with you, move an extra three squares forward. If they disagree, move back three squares. (Your turn is now finished, so if you have now landed on another sentence you may not give an opinion on its correctness.)

6. If you land on a blank square, you simply stay where you are until your next turn. If you land on a square where another person's counter is already standing, move on one square. This rule applies whether you land on a sentence or on a blank square.

7. At your next turn, move the counter the number of squares shown on the die. For example, if you are on square 16 and the die shows five dots, move your counter to square 21.

8. Each player proceeds the same way, starting always at square 1 (START).

9. To finish, you must land directly on square 70. If you are on square 68 and throw a six, count two forward and four back to land on square 66 (and hope you throw a four on your next turn).

# THROW A CONVERSATION

**Unit VIII / FUN AND GAMES / Level: High intermediate / Time: 20 minutes**

**Language Function(s):** Discussing a predetermined subject

**Materials:** One die per group of seven students

## In Class

1. Write the following table on the board. Divide the class into groups of seven (if possible) and explain the game to them. Tell them that they are going to discuss a subject. Throws of the dice will determine how long the discussion will be, what the subject will be, what their attitude toward it will be, and how many students will take part.

| Throw | Time in minutes | Subject | Personal attitude | Number |
|---|---|---|---|---|
| ⚀ | 1 | parents | proud | 7 |
| ⚁ | 2 | food | aggressive | 6 |
| ⚂ | 3 | home | shy | 5 |
| ⚃ | 4 | foreign languages | happy | 4 |
| ⚄ | 5 | us | sad | 3 |
| ⚅ | 6 | work | stern | 2 |

2. Explain that one student throws the die. The number he or she throws determines the time in minutes the discussion will take, that is, ⚄ means five minutes. The next student throws to determine the subject. ⚂ , for example, means home. The third student throws to determine the personal attitude of the students to the topic; for example ⚀ means proud. The next student throws to determine the number of participants the conversation will have, for example ⚅ means two. This student also chooses those to be involved. Using the above throws as an example, we see that two selected students have to speak for five minutes about home, in a proud way.

3. While the selected students hold their conversation, the others should listen to make sure that they do not deviate from the subject. The language should also be checked and the listeners should note whether or not the mood is appropriate. One of the listeners should be appointed as time-keeper. After each conversation the students who did not participate should be asked to comment on what they heard. About two or three rounds of the game should be enough for each lesson. Keep in the background, yourself, as much as possible, but keep a close watch on what is going on.

*Christine Frank*

**104**

# BLIND MAN'S BUFF

**Unit VIII / FUN AND GAMES / Level: Beginners to intermediate / Time: 20 minutes**

**Language Function(s):** Giving instructions

**Materials:**     Blindfolds; you also need a large room where the students can move about

## In Class

1. Teach or review with the class the following terms and concepts: *left, right, straight on, stop, turn around,* plus any other vocabulary you feel will be useful for the activity. This will, to a large extent, depend on the level of the class.

2. Move most of the furniture away from the center of the room but leave several objects such as chairs or small tables in the middle to serve as obstacles. Divide the class into pairs and tell the students to stand around the sides of the room, well away from the center. One partner in each pair is to put on a blindfold. The other plays the part of the guide.

3. The object of the game is to direct one's partner to the opposite side of the room without his or her touching any of the furniture or any of the other students. The guide gives directions using the vocabulary mentioned in step 1. On reaching the other side, partners swap roles (and the blindfold). It is now the original guide's turn to be guided while the other partner gives the directions.

4. A scoring system can be used if you think the students would like one. Award one point to the guide every time the "blind person" disobeys an instruction and hits something, and one point to the "blind person" when the guide gives him or her a false instruction resulting in a collision.

## Author's Note

This is a simplified version of the classic game "Airport."

*Joanna Sancha*

# VIII-11 ISLAND GAME

> **Unit VIII / FUN AND GAMES / Level: Intermediate / Time: 30−50 minutes**

**Language Function(s):** Comparing and justifying decisions; exchanging information

**Materials:** Copies of a map outline as described below.

## Before Class

Prepare copies of the outline of an imaginary island drawn on a grid with numbers going down and letters across, so that the points on the map can be easily referred to, for example A5 or C3. Either use the example on the next page or draw your own island.

## In Class

1. Brainstorm details that can be found on maps, such as rivers, resorts, industrial areas, roads, airports, nature reserves, tourist attractions, cities, forests, and so on. Make a list on the board.

2. Divide the class into pairs and give each pair a copy of the map. Ask each pair to fill in their maps together, discussing where to put such features as have already been mentioned in step 1. Students should use the map to build up the picture of a whole society. Encourage them to name the island and the cities, specify the natural resources etc. The more details they include, the more interesting the exercise becomes. Each pair may decide whether its map is large scale or small scale. Some may view it

as an entire nation, others as just a speck in the sea. Circulate, correcting mistakes, asking students to explain what they have filled in and providing help with the language as necessary.

3. Give each pair another blank map. Then seat each pair opposite another, and ask the two pairs to exchange information about their respective islands. The information should be dictated and the blanks filled in with the details of the opposite pair's map but *without looking at it*. This is made possible by using the reference grid, for example: "A river flows from A2 to D3, passing through B2 and C3." "There's a small industrial park just south of the capital, which is in the middle of D2." Only when all the information has been taken down may the one pair see the other's map. Invite discussion and comparison of the original and the attempted copy. If necessary cut the activity before all the details have been copied. Don't let the exchange go on too long so that it becomes boring. Finish with a short general discussion.

*Randal Holme*

## VIII-11 ISLAND GAME (continued)

**Unit VIII / FUN AND GAMES / Level: Low intermediate and above / Time: 15—30 minutes**

**Language Function(s):** Writing Sentences

**Materials:** None

## In Class

1. Tell the class they are going to make a sentence tree. Explain that because it is easier to read down than up, the tree will be inverted—upside down. (A sample tree is at the end of the recipe) Put a diagram on the board like this:

Tell the class that they will be adding words, putting out new branches after each word (until they have eight branches—see Section 8 below) to make sentences. The sentences should be as long as possible. Explain that the students will be working in teams, with members from each team taking turns at the board. Point out that team members will be penalized for adding words that cannot make a sentence, and add any other scoring rules you wish (see section 7 below).

2. Divide the class into two teams, A and B. Each team will take turns sending members up to the board one by one. Each student should go to the board at least once.

3. Ask one of the members of Team A to start by writing a word which could be the beginning of a sentence on the board. This word should be written as high on the board as possible, in the center, and the writer should have at least two sentences in mind that could start with it. After the word has been written, the writer draws two "branches" down from it, like this:

**The**

4. Now have Team B send someone to the board to write a word for each branch—and draw in two new branches under each word. Before sitting down, this person should read aloud the two partial sentences he or she has created.

5. Additions are made by another member of Team A, to create a total of eight branches. Further additions, by members of Teams A and B alternately, involve adding words to the existing branches without creating new branches. Each member should add a word to each of the branches that is still incomplete. Each member should read aloud all the sentences or sentence fragments to which he or she has contributed.

6. Each group should check the other's performance and should challenge anything that is considered inappropriate. When challenged, a writer must give an acceptable sentence (or sentences) he or she had in mind when writing. This rule should be applied strictly to avoid non-sentences or sentences that are grammatically incorrect.

7. Keep score, or appoint a class member from each team to do so. With more advanced groups you may wish to give bonus points for the appropriate use of conjunctions or relative pronouns, thus rewarding the formation of complex sentences. You may also wish to take points off for each mistake, for being forced to "pass" (in which case the other group sends up its next member) or for finishing a sentence (thus rewarding the formation of longer sentences). The rules you set will depend on how competitive you want to make the task.

8. Restrictions

    a. Note that you may have to limit the number of branches according to the level of your group. In any event I would suggest you restrict them to an absolute number of eight or the exercise may get out of control. For advanced groups capable of producing very long sentences, an overhead projector with a rolling transparency would be ideal if you have one.

b. If you wish, you can restrict the choice of first words, for example to, question words or auxiliaries where these need practice. You may also wish to specify that a particular word or structure be used.

9. Variations

a. With smaller classes it may be better to make this a collective exercise, rather than dividing the class into teams. In this case, let the students call out their words to you, or better still, to a "secretary" who writes them on the board.

b. Once the group is familiar with the rules, you can let them work in pairs. This can be made more competitive, if you wish, by rewarding the pair with the shortest, longest, or most complex sentence(s). Working in pairs may also be used to help individual students in a particular area of grammar, for example the use of auxiliaries in questions or negatives.

## Sample Tree

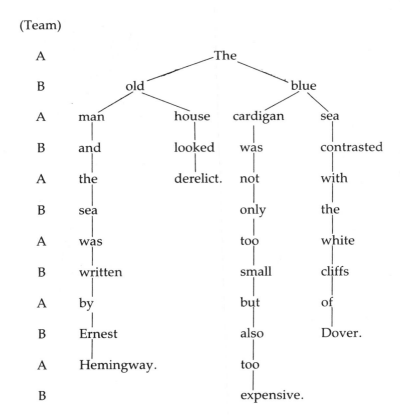

| (Team) | | | | |
|---|---|---|---|---|
| A | | The | | |
| B | old | | blue | |
| A | man | house | cardigan | sea |
| B | and | looked | was | contrasted |
| A | the | derelict. | not | with |
| B | sea | | only | the |
| A | was | | too | white |
| B | written | | small | cliffs |
| A | by | | but | of |
| B | Ernest | | also | Dover. |
| A | Hemingway. | | too | |
| B | | | expensive. | |

## Author's Note

I should like to acknowledge that I got this idea from one of my students, who had played a similar game at school.

*Peter Schimkus*

109

# VIII-13 GENERATING EXPRESSIONS

**Unit VIII / FUN AND GAMES / Level: Low intermediate and above / Time: 5−10 minutes**

**Language Function(s):** Creating idiomatic expressions

**Materials:** None

## Before Class

Select an expression such as "She's the apple of her father's eye" which has already been used and/or discussed in your class.

## In Class

1. Draw three columns on the board. For this expression the first column is for different sorts of fruits, the second for family members, and the third for parts of the body. Elicit items from the students and write them in the respective columns, for example:

| Fruit | Family | Part of Body |
|-------|--------|--------------|
| pear | sister | stomach |
| strawberry | cousin | head |
| banana | uncle | elbow |

And so on . . .

Build up a collection of eight to ten words in each column. Let the students explain any new words to each other as far as possible.

2. Coax the group into remembering the expression you selected before class and write it above the word lists. Ask the group why the expression should be specifically "the apple of the father's eye." Are there no other possibilities that are equally descriptive? What about some combinations from the three lists you have collected? Ask the students to read across (or diagonally across) the columns to form new possibilities such as: "She's the apricot of her nephew's knee."

3. A variation for lower levels is to base the activity on typical British pub names. (With students unfamiliar with such names, you should write several on the board, either real or ficticious.) "The Bishop's Finger," for example, would generate suggestions based on a combination of professions and parts of the body, say: "The Nurse's Ankle" or "The Engineer's Eye." (Higher levels could do these exercises as a lead-in to more serious work, perhaps a project on the origin of English and American sayings and "folk" names for places or objects.) Of course most of the variations generated are ridiculous, but then so are the originals—unless you find out where they came from. Moreover, the bizarre nature of the exercise is easily justified by the fact that it is such fun, presenting a really amusing means of waking up a drooping class.

*Christopher Sion*

**110**

# RIDDLE SCRAMBLE

**Unit VIII / FUN AND GAMES / Level: Low intermediate and above / Time: 10 minutes**

**Language Function(s):** Analyzing and combining questions and answers

**Materials:** Small cards (3″ × 5″ or 4″ × 6″ index or file cards, for example)

## Before Class

a. Select some riddles appropriate to the level of your class. It is important that the students understand the vocabulary or the humor will be lost on them. For classes of up to ten or twelve students pick out one riddle per person. For larger classes it is probably better to have two or three sets of riddles, e.g. two sets of eight for a class of sixteen. You can find some examples at the end of this recipe. Note that two of these depend on homonyms, words that sound the same but have different meanings and, in this case, spellings.

b. Draw horizontal lines on each card to divide it into four equal sections. The four sections correspond to the question and answer parts of two riddles. Label them Q, A, Q, A. Write the question part of one riddle in the top Q section and the answer part of another in the bottom A section of each card, as shown in the example. Arrange the material so that the missing part of each riddle is to be found on another card. This is not really as complicated as it sounds!

Example:

| Q: How do you know there's an elephant in your icebox? |
| --- |
| A: |
| Q: |
| A: The road. |

| Q: What goes from New York to L.A. without moving? |
| --- |
| A: |
| Q: |
| A: Because the others are week days. |

| Q: Why are Saturday and Sunday strong? |
| --- |
| A: |
| Q: |
| A: Footprints in the butter! |

Make sure that the riddles are split up so that each student has to ask *two* others in order to complete his or her card.

## In Class

1. Explain the activity to the class. Tell them they must find the missing questions and answers. (I do not usually tell them they are working with riddles,

which are supposed to be funny. I just wait for the light to dawn.) Make sure the students understand that they have *two separate* questions and answers. Encourage them to say the questions and answers out loud. They should not simply show their cards to the others.

2. Give each student a card. Tell them to wander about, asking questions and trying out their answers until

**111**

they make the proper connections. They should fill in the cards when they have found the correct question or answer. Provide help with vocabulary as required, but stay in the background as much as possible so that the students may work things out for themselves.

3. Get students to ask their riddles of others who do not know the answers. A further, optional, activity is to tell the class to put their cards away and reconstruct the riddles from memory. You will need to circulate to make sure they are correct.

## Riddles

What can you have after someone has taken it? Your snapshot.

Why do birds fly South for the winter? It's quicker than walking.

What goes from New York to L.A. without moving? The road.

What's white outside, green inside, and jumps? A frog sandwich.

Why are Saturday and Sunday strong? Because the others are week (weak) days.

Why can you always find something to eat in the desert? Because of the sandwiches (sand which is) there.

Why is an empty pocket book always the same? Because there's never any change in it.

Where does Friday come before Thursday? In the dictionary.

What can you hold without touching it? Your breath.

What gets bigger the more you take away from it? A hole.

Why did Bill take a tape measure to bed? He wanted to see how long he slept.

What animal can jump higher than a house? All of them. A house can't jump.

How do you know there's an elephant in your icebox? Footprints in the butter!

*Heidi Yorkshire*

Unit VIII / FUN AND GAMES / Level: Low intermediate and above /
Time: 15–30 minutes

**Language Function(s):** Asking questions

**Materials:** None

## In Class

1. Select two* talkative students and tell them to come out of the room with you to prepare an activity. Ask the others to remain quietly in class. This stage should only take a couple of minutes.

2. Tell the two students to imagine that they have had a dream that they cannot remember**. Strange as it may seem, they both had the *same* dream. Make it clear that it is only a game and not some sort of sinister psychological test. Explain that the rest of the class *do* know the contents of the dream and will help the two remember it. Tell them to prepare questions about the dream to establish what happened. However, the rest of the class may only answer "Yes" or "No." Questions such as "Where did it happen?' are not acceptable and need to be replaced by "Did it happen in the United States?", "Was it in New York City?", and so on. Leave the two to prepare as many questions as they can and return to the classroom.

3. Tell the rest of the class what you have told the two selected students and explain how to respond to the questions, namely: Questions ending with the letters AEIOU or Y are to be answered "Yes," and those ending with consonants "No." The manner in which the dream develops depends entirely on the questions.

   For example:

   Was it a nightmar*e*? (Yes)

Was it a bad drea*m*? (No)

Did I see a member of my famil*y*? (Yes)

Did I know the perso*n*? (No)

Was the girl prett*y*? (Yes)

Was the girl beautifu*l*? (No)

It is vitally important that this system is understood before the questions begin.

4. Call the two "dreamers" back into the room and tell them to ask their questions. The bizarre answers are easily explained by pointing out that it is only a dream. Dreams do not follow the logic of everyday life. Should the activity not get off the ground, or should the questioners lose inspiration you may prompt them by saying, for instance: "Why not ask what you were wearing?" or "You could try asking about where you were and who else was there." If the questioners do not manage to "crack the code" draw the game to a close before it goes on too long.

5. Follow up the activity by asking the "dreamers" what they felt, what they found particularly confusing, why they repeated questions over and over, and so on. If the group is interested you might continue with a discussion centered on recent dreams, recurring dreams, the psychology of dreams and related topics.

## Author's Notes

1. *It is also possible to do this activity with three or even four students asking the questions. However, it is not advisable to select only one student as it

**113**

tends to isolate him or her from the class and creates too much pressure to think of questions.

2. **This activity can by turned into a more specific exercise by focusing it on something relevant to your class, say: You had a dream about a bank/your job/a hospital/a new engineering project or whatever.

3. I should like to acknowledge that I originally got this idea from Susan Davies at Pilgrims in 1976.

*Christopher Sion*

# INDEX

# NOTES